Berlitz

ITALIAN LAKES

POCKET GUIDE

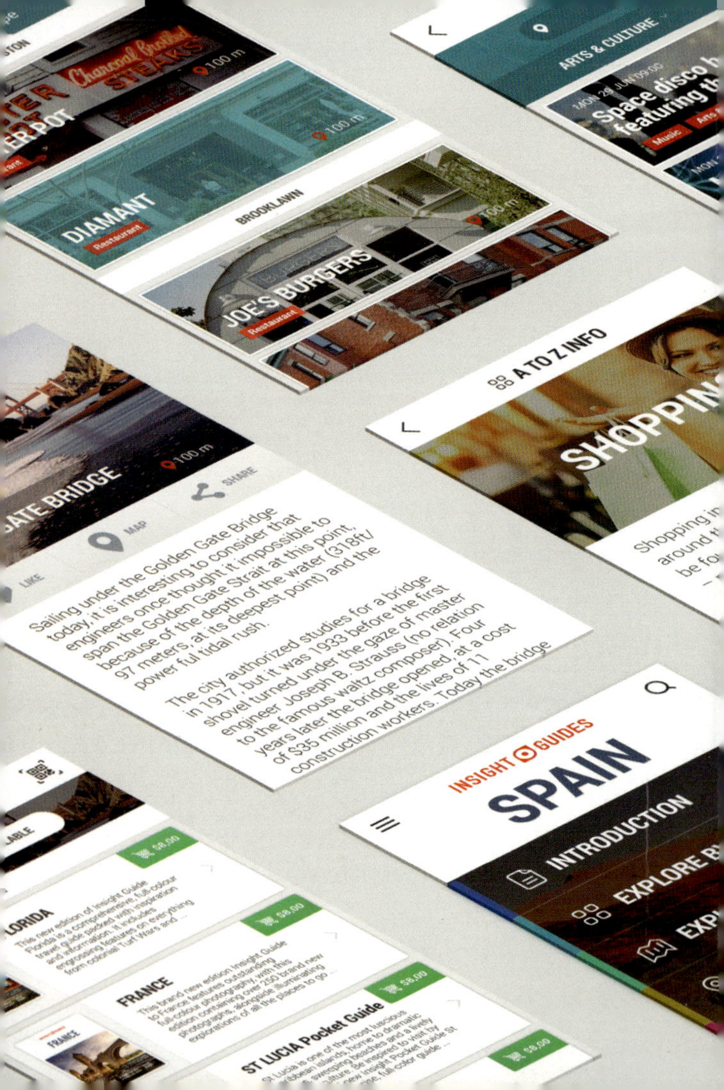

Charcoal Broiled
STEAKS
100 m
100 m
DIAMANT
Restaurant
BROOKLAWN
100 m
JOE'S BURGERS
Restaurant
ARTS & CULTURE
MON 29 JUN 09:00
Space disco h
featuring th
Music
Arts
A TO Z INFO
SHOPPIN
Shopping in
around
be fo
ATE BRIDGE
100 m
LIKE
MAP
SHARE
Sailing under the Golden Gate Bridge today, it is interesting to consider that engineers once thought it impossible to span the Golden Gate Strait at this point, because of the depth of the water (318ft/97 meters, at its deepest point) and the power ful tidal rush.
The city authorized studies for a bridge in 1917, but it was 1933 before the first shovel turned under the gaze of master engineer Joseph B. Strauss (no relation to the famous waltz composer). Four years later the bridge opened, at a cost of $35 million and the lives of 11 construction workers. Today the bridge
INSIGHT GUIDES
SPAIN
INTRODUCTION
EXPLORE B
EXP
$8.00
LORIDA
This new edition of Insight Guide Florida is a comprehensive, full-colour travel guide packed with inspiration and information. It includes engrossing features on everything from colonial Turf Wars and ...
$8.00
FRANCE
This brand new edition Insight Guide to France features outstanding full-colour photography, with this edition containing over 250 brand new photographs, alongside illuminating explorations of all the places to go ...
$8.00
ST LUCIA Pocket Guide
St Lucia is one of the most luscious Caribbean islands, home to dramatic sweeping beaches and a lively culture. Be inspired to visit by new Insight Pocket Guide St full-color guide ...
$8.00
FRANCE

TOP 10 ATTRACTIONS

MALCESINE

The picturesque fishing village lies at the foot of Monte Baldo. See page 56.

SANTA CATERINA DEL SASSO

This enchanting church convent clings to a cliff face above Lake Maggiore. See page 34.

VILLA DEL BALBIANELLO

Built in 1787 for an eccentric cardinal, it embodies the effortless style and beauty of the region. See page 42.

VILLA CARLOTTA

Famed for its sumptuous gardens, it sits on Lake Como's western shore. See page 44.

SIRMIONE

With a dramatic 13th-century castle, it is one of Lake Garda's most visited resorts. See page 49.

VERONA'S ROMAN ARENA

Once the scene of gladiatorial combat, it now stages operatic extravaganzas. See page 75.

THE BORROMEO ISLANDS

A suitably grandiose home for a flock of peacocks. See page 28.

VILLA TARANTO

Its botanical gardens are planted with around 20,000 different species of trees, shrubs and flowers. See page 32.

BERGAMO'S CITTÀ ALTA

Packed with magnificent medieval and Renaissance monuments. See page 65.

BELLAGIO

The 'pearl of Lake Como' enjoys unrivalled panoramic mountain views. See page 45.

A PERFECT DAY IN

8.00am

Breakfast

Take breakfast in your hotel or join the locals with a cappuccino and *cornetto* (croissant) in a lakeview café.

10.00am

Baroque extravaganza

Head for Stresa's ferry station at Piazza Marconi, buy a ticket that includes admission to the island sights and hop on one of the regular ferries going north to Ancona. Alight at the first stop, Isola Bella, the Borromean princes' summer residence. Explore the sumptuously decorated Palazzo Borromeo, and the beguiling, ship-shaped terraces of gardens, complete with statues and peacocks.

11.30am

Fisherman's Island

Catch the next ferry for a five-minute hop across to the tiny Isola dei Pescatori (also called Isola Superiore) with its pretty fishing village. Stroll through its tiny alleys, strung with fishing nets, then lunch on fish fresh from the lake at one of the hotel restaurants, soaking up the views from a lakeside terrace. Alternatively, enjoy a picnic on the pebble beach.

1.45pm

Isola Madre

Most boats en route to Isola Madre call at Baveno, a quieter version of Stresa, set below a pink granite mountain. Stay on the boat for the ten-minute crossing from here to Isola Madre, the largest, and once the wildest, of the Borromean islands. Stroll through gently landscaped gardens, with their profusion of exotic trees and shrubs, then make a brief visit to the villa, which is noticeably subdued after Palazzo Borromeo.

THE ITALIAN LAKES

3.00pm

Monte Mottarone

Catch the ferry across to Carciano and take a cable car ride to the Monte Mottarone peak (20 minutes), a natural balcony commanding magnificent views over the Alps and lakes. For the very finest views, which on a clear day encompass seven lakes, climb from the upper cable-car station for about 20 minutes to the summit, or take the chairlift.

5.00pm

Down the mountain

Descend to Stresa on the cable car or, for an adrenalin-fuelled ride, try the Alpyland Coaster with 2-seater bobs speeding down at up to 40kph (25mph). If time permits, alight halfway down at the Giardino Botanico Alpinia, the rock gardens with over 1,000 species of Alpine and medicinal plants.

6.30pm

Belle Époque grandeur

Follow in the footsteps of Ernest Hemingway and take an *aperitivo* in the palatial Grand Hotel des Iles Borromées overlooking the lake.

8.00pm

Wining and dining

Dine at Il Vicoletto (see page 106) or opt for one of the alfresco pizzerias, preferably with an open-fired oven, in the centre of the resort. After a leisurely dinner, end the evening with a lakeside stroll and a liqueur in a local bar.

CONTENTS

INTRODUCTION 10

A BRIEF HISTORY 15

WHERE TO GO 27

Lake Maggiore 27
Stresa and the Golfo Borromeo 27, Monte Mottarone 31, Verbania 32, Southern Lake Maggiore 34, Northern Lake Maggiore 35

Lake Como 37
Como Town 38, Ramo di Como 41, Centro Lago 44, Ramo di Colico 48

Lake Garda 48
The southern shores 49, The western shore 50, Garda Trentino 54

The eastern shore 56

Lesser lakes 59
Lake Orta 59, Varese and its lake 61, Lake Iseo 62

Lombard cities 65
Bergamo 65, Brescia 68, Cremona 71, Mantua 72

Verona 75
Piazza Brà and the Arena 76, Piazza delle Erbe 77, Piazza dei Signori and Arche Scaligere 77, La Casa di Giulietta 78, Churches and Roman Theatre 79, Castelvecchio and San Zeno Maggiore 81

WHAT TO DO 83

Sports and outdoor activities 83
Entertainment 86
Shopping 88
Children's lakes 92

EATING OUT 96

A–Z TRAVEL TIPS 114

RECOMMENDED HOTELS 134

DICTIONARY 143

INDEX 167

FEATURES

Getting round the lakes 10
Saint Carlo Borromeo (1538–84) 20
Historical landmarks 25
Sons of Como 39
Tignale and Tremósine 53
Limone's elixir of life 55
Monte Baldo 59
Visiting Verona 79
Torrone from Cremona 91
Lake trips by boat 93
Calendar of events 95
Coffee break 103

INTRODUCTION

Set among the southern foothills of the Alps, the Italian lakes extend over four different regions of northwest Italy: Piedmont, Lombardy, Trentino and the Veneto. The famous trio are Maggiore, Como and Garda, but there are also a number of smaller, peaceful lakes scattered among the valleys.

Each lake has its own character, whether it is tiny, jewel-like Orta, with its perfectly preserved medieval village and islet; beguiling Como where mountains plunge into the deep waters and picture-postcard villages cling to the slopes; vast and varied Garda – fjord-like in the north, sea-like in the south; or stately Maggiore, where snowcapped mountains form a dramatic backdrop to the enchanting Borromeo Islands. What they all have in common is a fertile shoreline, with a varied

GETTING ROUND THE LAKES

The main lakes see large numbers of holidaymakers from late spring to early autumn. Long stretches of the lakeside, including Como's eastern shore and much of Lake Maggiore's western one, are spoilt by heavy traffic on narrow and tortuous roads. While a car is clearly useful for touring, it is far more relaxing to base yourself in one lake resort and hop around by boat.

Ferries, hydrofoils and excursion cruisers provide excellent services linking almost all the towns and villages. Get up early and you can tour an entire lake, even one as big as Maggiore or Como, and have lunch on board the ferry. Cable cars, which climb to vantage points on the hillsides above the lakes, also offer some sensational views.

and exotic array of flora that thrives in the benign spring-to-autumn climate.

Toscalano-Maderno

VILLAS, GARDENS AND CASTLES

Sumptuous lakeside villas and their gardens, created originally for northern European nobility or well-heeled Milanese, are a major draw of the larger lakes. Como in particular has drawn the rich and famous, from Pliny the Younger who built villas at Bellagio to George Clooney who has a lakeside villa at Laglio. Palatial residences such as Como's Villa d'Este and Villa Serbelloni have been converted to luxury hotels, other villas and gardens throw their gates open to the public, and those in private hands can be admired from the lake as you chug past on a ferryboat.

Incongruous with the mountain settings, the lake shores are Riviera-like, studded with olive groves, palms and citrus trees; lakeside promenades are lined by palms and oleanders while throughout the spring a proliferation of azaleas, rhododendrons and camellias create a blaze of colour on the gently sloping banks.

Rising above the lakeshore villages are the lofty belltowers of Romanesque churches and the battlements of medieval castles. On Lake Garda the crenellated castles were the work of the power-hungry Scaligeri from Verona. Maggiore's fortifications and island palazzi were built by the Borromeo family of Milan

Latin lake names

The lakes are often referred to by their old Roman names: Verbano for Maggiore (after the verbena plant that flourished and still flourishes on its shores), Lario for Como, Benaco ('Beneficent') for Garda, Cusio for Lake Orta and Sebino for Lake Iseo.

– who to this very day own the islands and the lake's main castle at Angera.

A PLAYGROUND FOR THE RICH AND FAMOUS

As with every beautiful corner of Italy, the region is steeped in association with famous figures. In Roman times the poet Catullus owned a villa at Sirmione, Virgil was born near Mantua and the writer/historians Pliny the Elder and Pliny the Younger came from Como. Shelley, Wordsworth and other romantic poets were bewitched by the dramatic natural beauty of the deep-blue waters and mountain peaks. Shelley sung the praises of Lake Como: 'it surpasses in beauty everything I have ever seen hitherto'.

In the late-19th century the lakes became a pleasure ground for the rich, royal and famous. Queen Victoria stayed in Villa Cara at Baveno near Stresa in 1879; later the Grand Hotel in Gardone Riviera on Lake Garda hosted Somerset Maugham, Vladimir Nabokov and Winston Churchill. D.H. Lawrence, in describing Limone on Lake Garda, wrote of 'a lake as beautiful as the beginning of creation'. Hemingway, who was recuperating at Stresa's Grand Hotel des Iles Borromées after a WWI battle wound in 1918, used the resort as a backdrop in *A Farewell to Arms*.

Today's big names are soccer stars, Hollywood celebrities and Russian tycoons. The 'Clooney effect' (ie George's 25-room holiday home at Laglio) has sent property prices rocketing on the southwestern shores of Lake Como.

HISTORIC CITIES

The southern stretches of the region, typified by the flatlands of the Po and great swathes of industry, are also home to artistically rich cities such as Bergamo, Brescia, Mantua and Verona. In the heart of the cities (or in the case of Bergamo on top of the hill) there are fine historic centres bearing the marks of centuries of history. While Bergamo and Verona are immediately appealing, Mantua and Brescia are more of an acquired taste. Verona apart, these historic cities are comparatively free of crowds and commercialism, being bypassed by tourists making a beeline for Italy's more famous cities. Easily accessed from the lakes, they make ideal destinations for day trips.

Just an hour's train ride or drive from lakes Maggiore and Como, Milan is Italy's economic and cultural capital. Though famous for fashion, it has artistic riches too, among them the vast Gothic Duomo, Leonardo's *Last Supper* and the Brera art gallery.

Passenger ferry on Lake Como

WHICH LAKE?

The main resorts on Maggiore and Como have a comfortable genteel charm, attracting large numbers of older visitors (mainly British and German) who are content to enjoy the scenery from the lakeside promenade, take boat trips around the lakes, visit islands, gardens and lakeside villas, and take funicular rides to admire the views. On Lake Maggiore the grande dame resort of Stresa is the main place to stay, just a ferry hop from the Borromeo Islands. Upper Maggiore lies in Switzerland and although the resorts are Italian in feel, with their sunny piazzas and alfresco eateries, there is a marked Swiss efficiency about them. Lake Como, particularly popular with the British and Americans, is the most romantic of the lakes, offering dramatic scenery, picturesque villages, belle époque resorts and the beautiful village of Bellagio at the heart of the lake.

German-orientated Lake Garda generally attracts a younger crowd and is more suitable for families. There are sports, beaches and theme parks galore, and sufficient nightlife to keep the energetic entertained until the early hours. The lakes in general are a sporting paradise, offering water sports, hiking, mountain biking, skiing (in winter) and adventure sports. Lake Garda, with all those and more, is one big fitness centre. The *pelèr* (or *suer*) wind from the north, and the *ora* from the south, ensure superb sailing and windsurfing conditions, especially at the northern end of the lake. The mountains and ridges above the lakes offer endless opportunities for hikers and rock climbers; and for the less actively inclined there are cable cars up the slopes where you can enjoy some breathtaking views.

Then there is little Lake Orta, the only Italian lake lying entirely in Piedmont. The village of Orta San Giulio, overlooking the tiny Isola San Giulio, is arguably the most picturesque of any in the lakes and is certainly worthy of a detour from Lake Maggiore. Lake Iseo, between lakes Como and Garda, is more tranquil and less self-consciously quaint than the larger lakes.

A BRIEF HISTORY

This region's remarkable landscape was formed at the end of the last Ice Age when the Alpine glaciers retreated, leaving deep lake-filled valleys. For over 10,000 years people have also been leaving their mark here, from the prehistoric rock carvings at Val Camonica to the magnificent 17th- and 18th-century villas that surround Lake Como. The region's location on trade routes between Rome and central Europe played a crucial role in its history, ensuring prosperity, but also luring a succession of foreign invaders.

EARLY SETTLERS

Lombardy and the lakes lie within a larger area that the Romans called Gallia Cisalpina ('Gaul this side of the Alps'), a vast wild tract of land and lakes. Gallic tribes, pushing south from the Rhine Valley, were inhabiting the fertile plains of the Po Valley by the 4th century BC, creating their settlements at what are now Milan, Brescia, Verona, Mantua, Bergamo and Como. In 224 BC the Romans put an end to these Celtic forays by conquering the area south of

Pope Leo I

Roman relics

The most conspicuous legacies of Roman rule are Brescia's Capitoline Temple and Roman theatre and Verona's superbly preserved arena, the third largest surviving from ancient times.

the Po, and just a year later Flaminius crossed the river, dismantled its bridges and defeated all of the Celtic tribes, including the powerful Insubres.

However, during the Second Punic War and its aftermath, when the Romans were more concerned with defeating Hannibal, the Gauls rose up again, attacking the Roman fortresses on the River Po. Consular armies were despatched north, defeating the tribes at the River Mincio near Mantua. A further victory near Lake Como finally obliged the Gauls to sue for peace. With the final reduction of Cisalpine Gaul, the Celtic tribes were progressively merged with the Romans.

HUNS, GOTHS AND LOMBARDS

By the 3rd century AD Cisalpine Gaul had become a commercially prosperous region of the Roman Empire and an important gateway to northern Europe. Attila the Hun, invading his way through Italy, plundered and pillaged Milan, Verona, Bergamo and Brescia in AD 452, but after the mediation of Pope Leo I, the infamous barbarian warrior halted at the Po and promised never to return.

Following the breakdown of the Western Roman Empire in 476 the region was subject to further waves of invaders. The German Odoacer crowned himself king at Pavia but was later vanquished by Theodoric the Ostrogoth. During his 40-year reign Theodoric ruled through surviving Roman institutions, welding together Goths and Romans, administering justice, and creating fine buildings, including a palace for himself in Verona on the site of the present-day Castelvecchio.

The Lombards, a warfaring Germanic tribe, descended on the region, putting an end to any vestige of political unity that may have survived the Roman era. They crossed the Alps in the spring of 568, and two years later they had conquered all the main cities north of the Po, with the exception of Pavia, seat of the royal palace. Their kingdom in Italy lasted a couple of centuries and was in the main ruled by the king and his royal officials who kept a check on the power of the dukes and counts. The Lombards were eventually absorbed into the Italian population, adopting Roman life and customs, freely intermarrying and, in many cases, converting to Christianity. Ethnically and socially they left an indelible mark on the people of northern Italy.

Invasion of papal territories by the Lombards forced the pope to appeal for support from Pepin, the Christian king of the Franks. In 774 Pepin's son Charlemagne and his army conquered much of Italy, including the north, and took the Lombard crown. On Christmas Day 800 Pope Leo III revived the Roman imperial title when he crowned Charlemagne Holy Roman Emperor. However, the Franks failed to establish a durable state in Italy and in 1024 the royal palace

Charlemagne being crowned Holy Roman Emperor

at Pavia, symbol of the power of the Holy Roman Empire, was destroyed by the local people.

ERA OF THE COMMUNES

The early 11th century saw the emergence of the commune, or free city-state, the quintessential institution of medieval northern Italy. Prior to this, local aristocrats and the emerging commercial classes had been prepared to play second fiddle to the state in exchange for a degree of patronage from the emperor or king. As the rulers' power and influence waned, the strength and independence of the aristocrats and tradesmen increased.

As a consequence, economic and de facto governmental power passed to the localities, giving birth to the communes. These were self-governing municipal institutions with their origins in rebellion, treaty or charter. Typical rights included the control of justice, personal liberty of the townsmen and powers to regulate trade and levy local taxes and tolls. Milan acquired communal status in 1045, followed later by Brescia, Como, Bergamo, Verona and Mantua.

Castello Scaligero

These communes were vulnerable to factional feuds, with powerful families often grouping together and gobbling up rival city-states. The great ideological conflict between the papacy and the Holy Roman Empire gave further impetus to conflict when these 'superpowers' vied for support in the northern cities. Within each city-state rival families adopted the labels 'Guelph' for the papacy and 'Ghibelline' for the empire. The famous vendetta in Verona between Montagues (Ghibellines) and Capulets (Guelphs) is just one example.

The Scaligeri

The ruthless and tyrannical Scaligeri dynasty ruled Verona from 1260 to 1387. A number of their castles, all with characteristic fishtail battlements, can be seen around Lake Garda (Castello Scaligero at Malcesine is a good example) and their elaborate Gothic mausoleums still stand in central Verona (see page 75).

THE GREAT DYNASTIES

The 13th century saw a shift in territorial and city-state power. The main cities fell to despotic rulers: Milan to the Visconti, Mantua to the Bonacolsi, Verona to the della Scalas (or Scaligeri). By the mid-14th century the smaller cities had lost their independent communal status. Milan had swallowed up great swathes of northern Italy and by 1402 had even extended its territories south to Tuscany.

As well as able administrators, the family dynasties were dynamic patrons of the arts. Milan and Mantua, which was by now under the civilizing rule of the Gonzagas, were great centres of art, drawing the leading artists, poets and scholars of the time. Under the mighty Visconti dynasty, cathedrals, fortresses and palazzi were constructed across the region, among them the cathedrals of Milan and Como and the Certosa (Charterhouse) of Pavia. Ludovico il Moro of the Sforza family, who inherited Milan from the Visconti, attracted Bramante, the great High

Renaissance architect and decorative painter; and Leonardo da Vinci, who produced most of his ground-breaking artistic, scientific and medical studies here. The Mantuan court drew the great Florentine architect, Alberti, and the painter, Mantegna, who glorified the Gonzaga family in his brilliant fresco decorations. Verona produced the great Renaissance artist, Veronese, and celebrated architects such as Sanmicheli; Brescia produced its own school of painters; Bergamo played host to a whole range of painters from the workshops of Milan and Venice, and saw

SAINT CARLO BORROMEO (1538–84)

Born into the Borromeo dynasty (who to this day own Lake Maggiore's Borromeo islands, the castle at Angera and the fishing rights of the entire lake), the ascetic Carlo became a leading light in the Catholic Counter-Reformation. He was born in the (now ruined) castle of Arona on the southern shores of Lake Maggiore and devoted his life to the reform and welfare of the church.

Appointed cardinal and Archbishop of Milan by his uncle, Pope Pius IV, Carlo founded seminaries and colleges for the education of clerical and lay members, rid Milan's Duomo of all its ornamentation, paid regular visits to hundreds of parishes and worked ceaselessly during the plague of 1576–8 to accommodate the sick and bury the dead.

However, political turmoil beset him as he became embroiled in disputes with the governor and senate, and faced rebellion from various religious orders. In 1569 members of the order of the Humiliati (Brothers of Humility) hatched an unsuccessful conspiracy to take his life. Carlo was canonised posthumously by Pope Paul V in 1610.

the creation of the Colleoni Chapel, a masterpiece of the Lombard Renaissance.

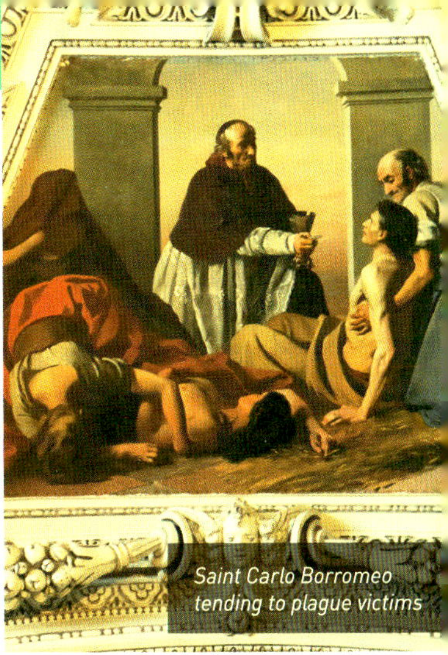
Saint Carlo Borromeo tending to plague victims

From the early 1400s the republic of Venice, until then an exclusively maritime power, with naval bases from the lagoon to Constantinople, had begun to extend her net into the hinterland. Starting with Verona in 1405, huge swathes of territory were taken by military conquest from Milan, including Brescia and Bergamo, to extend the Venetian Empire to the River Adda. In 1454 the war was ended by the Peace of Lodi and an Italian league was formed, made up of the two dominant powers in the area, Milan and Venice, plus Florence.

FOREIGN INTERVENTION

In the late 15th and early 16th centuries, the small duchies that made up Italy became a battleground in the struggle between France and Habsburg Spain, the two great powers of the age. In the aftermath of the 1525 Battle of Pavia, when the French were expelled from the Duchy of Milan, treaties with the pope settled the future of Italy for the next two centuries. The state of Milan was restored to the Sforza dynasty, but on the death of Francesco II in 1535 it fell under the domination of the Spanish Habsburg Emperor, Charles V, who later granted the duchy to his son, the future Philip II of Spain. Spanish rule

Battle of Solferino, 1859

was to endure until 1706. Venice on the other hand, with its increased territorial domains, maintained its independence. The Gonzaga rule of Mantua survived the territorial aggrandisements of both Milan and Venice, and the ruling family continued as masters of Mantua until the early 18th century.

In Spanish northern Italy the kaleidoscope of dynastic and interstate struggle gave way to a period of economic stagnation and political decline. Executive power was in the hands of a governor, assisted by a senate, but important directives came from Madrid. The Italian aristocratic and bourgeois classes lost their political and commercial vigour and the effects were compounded by military levies and requisitions in support of Spanish wars, inflation, famine and plague.

During the War of Spanish Succession (1702–13) Austria seized control of most of northern Italy, including the Lakes. In 1796, following his victories in Piedmont, Napoleon swept into Lombardy, and the northern cities became part of the short-lived Cisalpine Republic, allied with France. At the close of the Napoleonic wars Lombardy was restored to Austria, under the Congress of Vienna.

Austrian rule, which if anything was disliked even more than that of Spain, finally came to an end when Camillo Cavour, the architect of Italian unification, decided that the only way of defeating Austria was with the support of France. In 1859 two thousand French troops were moved by rail into northern Italy under the command of Napoleon III. The Austrians were defeated first at Magenta, west of Milan, and then at Solferino, close to Lake Garda, this time with the help of Italian troops who either fought with the French or deserted the Austrian side. Some 40,000 men perished in the battle, inspiring the Swiss humanitarian, Henri Durant, who witnessed the carnage, to found the International Red Cross. The battles of Magenta and Solferino can be seen as a watershed in the military campaign for the unification of Italy – which was finally achieved in 1871.

20TH CENTURY AND BEYOND

Rapid growth and industrialisation characterised the post-unification period. Milan became the economic and cultural capital of Italy and over 50 years the population trebled in size. It was in Milan that Mussolini created the Fasci di Combattimento in 1919, the nucleus of the National Fascist Party. Following the fall of the socialist regime, Mussolini put Lake Garda on the political map by setting up his puppet republic in Salò in 1943, under the protection of a German army. In April 1945, just before the Allies reached Milan, Il Duce was finally captured at Dongo on Lake Como as he tried to flee to Switzerland. The following day he was executed along with 15 Nazi officials and his mistress, Clara Petacci. Their bodies were strung by their feet from the girders of a petrol station in Milan's Piazzale Loreto.

Following widespread destruction in World War II, Milan and the Lombard cities saw major reconstruction and rapid economic recovery. Milan became an industrial powerhouse, forming, with Genoa and Turin, the 'industrial triangle' of Italy.

The city has emerged as Italy's leading centre for commerce, finance and fashion. But alongside the economic boom came political scandal, organised crime and terrorism. In the early 1990s Milan was the focus of the great political scandal dubbed *Tangentopoli* (Bribesville). Extensive investigations, known as the *Mani Pulite* (Clean Hands), exposed political corruption on a massive scale.

BERLUSCONI'S RISE, FALL AND RISE AGAIN?

Among the accused in the *Mani Pulite* was Italy's media magnate, Silvio Berlusconi. The controversial and colourful billionaire was elected to his second spell as Prime Minister in 2001 on a tide of populism and nationalism, with a pledge to reform the economy. The country's longest serving post-war Prime Minister, he continues to dominate Italian politics, serving three terms so far. But his career has been dogged by sex and corruption scandals and his government led Italy to the brink of financial disaster. The 75-year old resigned in November 2011, after losing his parliamentary majority in a vote on austerity measures to cut the country's spiralling debt of €1.9 trillion.

Berlusconi's successors Mario Monti, Enrico Letta and the Democratic Party's young and energetic leader Matteo Renzi all failed to pass significant changes. Renzi's ambitious constitutional reforms package was rejected in a 2016 referendum, leading to his resignation and a new period of political uncertainty.

The 2018 elections led to a hung parliament, which at the time of writing remains unresolved. Berlusconi's Forza Italia party (reformed in 2013) came fourth with 14% of the vote. With his six-year ban from office following a conviction for tax fraud being overturned in May 2018, the way is paved for Berlusconi to run for a fourth term as Italy's Prime Minister.

HISTORICAL LANDMARKS

c.8000 BC–3rd century BC Inhabitants of the Val Camonica, north of Lake Iseo, leave thousands of carvings on the rocks, illustrating prehistoric life.

202–191 BC Romans start to establish colonies in Milan, Como, Brescia, Verona and other settlements.

222 BC Romans conquer Milan (Mediolaum).

AD 286 Milan becomes capital of the Western Roman Empire.

313 Constantine grants religious freedom to Christians in Milan.

568 Lombards invade Po Valley and lakes.

774 Charlemagne brings Lombard rule to an end.

11th century Emergence of the communes or city-states.

1118–27 Como defeated by Milan in the Ten Years War.

12th–15th century Milan ruled by the Viscontis and Sforzas; Lake Garda and Verona by the Scaligeri (della Scala) dynasty.

16th century Milan and the western lakes controlled by Spanish, the eastern lakes by the Venetian Empire.

1714 Spain cedes Lombardy to Austria.

1796 Napoleon invades. Milan becomes capital of the Cisalpine Republic.

1814–70 The Risorgimento – liberation and political unification of Italy.

1859 French defeat Austrians in the battles of Magenta and Solferino.

1870 Italy is unified under King Vittorio Emanuele II.

1921 Mussolini founds the National Fascist Party in Milan.

1943–5 Mussolini is installed as head of a puppet republic at Salò, Lake Garda. In 1945 he and his mistress, Claretta Petacci, are executed.

2001 Silvio Berlusconi is elected Prime Minister.

2002 The euro replaces the lira as the official Italian currency.

2011 The 150th anniversary of Italian Unification. Silvio Berlusconi steps down as Prime Minister. Mario Monti heads a new national unity government.

2014 Democratic Party's Matteo Renzi forms a new government.

2017 People vote for greater autonomy in non-binding referendums in Veneto and Lombardy.

2018 Elections lead to a hung parliament. Matteo Salvini, a right-wing Populist, becomes Deputy Prime Minister after receiving most votes.

Picturesque street in Bellagio, Lake Como

WHERE TO GO

It is worth devoting a couple of weeks in order to experience the lakes region and the historic Lombard cities fully. The A4 autostrada provides a quick way of getting across the region by car, but the roads around the lakes can be very slow going. If you are without a car or your time is limited to a week or less, make your base at one of the larger lake resorts and take one or two relaxing ferry trips around the lakeshore. The Roman and Renaissance delights of Verona warrant an overnight stay.

LAKE MAGGIORE

Famed for its jewel-like islands and mountain-girt northern shores, Maggiore is the second largest of the Italian lakes. Long and narrow, it snakes 65km (40 miles) from the Swiss canton of **Ticino** in the north to **Lombardy** in the south. The western shore, where most of the main resorts are located, lies in **Piedmont**. The most scenic section of the lake is the **Gulf of Borromeo**, named after the family who have had a monopoly on Maggiore's star attractions for four and a half centuries.

STRESA AND THE GOLFO BORROMEO

Stresa, 'Queen of the Lake', lies at the foot of the majestic **Mottarone peak** and boasts glorious views to the islands. Following the opening of the **Simplon Pass** in 1906, the town became a highly fashionable resort, with splendid belle-époque villas and gardens, sports clubs and a casino. Today, huge old-fashioned hotels line its immaculate, garden-lined promenade. Foremost amongst these is the sumptuous **Grand Hotel des Iles Borromées**, whose star-studded guest list has included

For love of the lake

According to Stendhal, 'when a man has a heart and a shirt he should sell the shirt in order to see Lake Maggiore'. Byron, Shelley, Flaubert, Ruskin and Dickens were among other literati who have sung the praises of the lake.

Queen Victoria, Churchill and Ernest Hemingway.

The resort may have lost the cachet it once enjoyed (today's visitors are more likely to be package tourists or conference delegates than royalty or celebrities) but as a base on the lake it still can't be beaten for views, excursions and easy access to the **Borromeo Islands** ❶ (Isole Borromee). It also has an appealing older quarter behind the waterfront where the narrow cobbled streets are lined by little shops and eateries, and the central, plane-shaded piazza buzzes with café life after dark.

From Stresa it's a quick ferry hop to **Isola Bella**, the first of the Borromeo Islands (www.borromeoturismo.it; late-Mar–late-Oct daily 9am–5.30pm; cumulative ticket available with Isola Madre). It was in the mid-16th century that Count Carlo III decided to transform the rocky islet (then known as Isola Inferiore) into a monumental baroque palace and gardens. He named it Isola Isabella after his wife, later shortened to Isola Bella (Beautiful Island). In the 17th century Carlo's son, Vitaliano, took over the project, commissioning leading architects and artists. It was not until 1959 however, that the scheme was finally complete.

Designed to give the impression of the prow of a grandiose vessel, the island creates a dramatic impact as you approach by boat. The palace, terraces and gardens occupy almost the entire island, leaving just a cluster of houses near the harbour and a few souvenir shops. The stern facade belies a lavish interior, full of gilt and stuccowork, marble statues and Murano chandeliers. A tour takes in the Sala di Napoleone (Napoleon's Room) where he and Josephine slept in 1797. At lake level there are six mosaic grottoes, built by the Borromeans to avoid the stifling summer heat.

The garden is a baroque extravaganza of statuary, exotic plants and flowers. The ten ornate terraces culminate in a huge statue of a unicorn – one of the Borromeo symbols. Even if you find the grounds unbearably pompous you can't fail to admire the remarkable variety of exotic flora, planned to create colour and scent from early spring to late autumn – not to mention the sublime views across to the Mottarone peak.

A five-minute ferry ride from Isola Bella brings you to **Isola dei Pescatori**, or – as you hear the ferry men announce it – 'Isola Superiore dei Pescatori'. The full name derives from the Latin

The garden terrace on Isola Bella

Visiting the islands

To see the Borromeo Islands at a leisurely pace, you should allow a whole day – though a longish morning or afternoon may suffice. Bear in mind that in season the islands are inundated with crowds – the earlier you set off the better – and beware of boat touts near the main ferry landing stage charging far higher prices than the ferries.

superior, indicating that it is further north than Isola Bella ('Isola Inferiore'). The quaint, picturesque and laid-back Fishermen's Island couldn't be more of a contrast to formal Isola Bella. Heralded by the spire of its church, it is no more than a cluster of simple fishermen's houses and narrow alleys. At the end of the 19th century the population was around 200 and visitors were a rarity. Today there are 50 permanent residents. Despite the summer influx of tourists the island manages to preserve fishing traditions and is a lovely spot to stop for lunch and try the fish fresh from the lake.

The ferry stops at **Baveno** before arriving at the second of the Borromeo islands: **Isola Madre** (same opening hours as Isola Bella, see page 28). Different again, this one is a thickly wooded island, where English-style gardens dominate. The island has belonged to the Borromeo family since the 1500s and the glorious gardens were designed in the 19th century on what was formerly hunting ground. Peacocks and pheasants roam freely among the rare plants and exotic flora. Renowned for azaleas, rhododendrons and camellias, the gardens also nurture banana plants and sugar cane, lemon trees, magnolia, a Ginkgo biloba and a 200-year old Kashmir cypress tree, reputedly the largest in Europe. The palace is far less grandiose than its sister on Isola Bella. The rooms have been reconstructed and the interior has a mixed collection of Borromeo portraits, baroque allegorical paintings, tapestries, porcelain and a puppet theatre.

MONTE MOTTARONE

Between lakes Maggiore and Orta, the **Mottarone peak** ❷ is a natural balcony commanding a wonderful panorama of the lakes and the Alps; on one of those rare clear days you are said to be able to see seven lakes. Access is either by car (the last section is a toll road owned by the Borromeo family), foot (four hours along marked trails) or via the Mottarone cable car on the north side of Stresa (www.stresa-mottarone.it; daily 9.30am–5.30pm). Half way up, the cable car stops at the **Giardino Botanico Alpinia** (Apr–early Oct daily 9.30am–6pm), an Alpine garden with over 1,000 species and fine lake views. The garden can also be reached by a minibus from Stresa. The Mottarone is also popular with hang gliders and mountain bikers (bikes and helmets can be rented). The latest attraction is the adjustable speed **Alpyland Coaster** (www.alpyland.com; Apr–Oct Mon–Fri 10am–5pm, Sat–Sun 10am–6pm, Nov–Mar weekends only) which enables you to bobsleigh down the mountain at speeds of up to 40kph (25 mph) come snow or sunshine.

Peacocks roam the gardens on Isola Madre

Monte Mottarone

On the southern edge of Stresa the **Villa Pallavicino** (www.parcopallavicino.it; mid-Mar–Sept daily 9am–7pm, last entry at 5.30pm, Oct–early Nov 9am–6pm, last entry at 4.30pm) has a 20-hectare (50-acre) park with botanical gardens and a collection of animals, some of which roam freely through the grounds. Only the gardens are open to the public.

Baveno is a smaller version of Stresa which became prosperous from the pink granite quarried from its slopes. This was used in Milan's Galleria Vittorio Emanuele II and St Paul's in Rome. Like Stresa, Baveno became fashionable in the 19th century, and in 1879 was visited by Queen Victoria. Rising above the village is the spire of the Church of Santi Gervasio e Protasio, which retains its Romanesque facade and an enchanting baptistery with frescoed vault and cupola.

VERBANIA

Facing Stresa across the Gulf of Borromeo, suburban **Verbania** was created by Mussolini in 1939 to unite several communities, including **Intra** and **Pallanza**. By far the prettiest of these is **Pallanza**, where magnolias and oleanders line the quaysides and colourful cafés flank the piazzas. The resort has some fine villas and gardens, such as the famous **Villa Taranto** ❸ (www.villataranto.it; Mar daily 8.30am–5.30pm, Apr–Sept until 6.30pm, Oct

9am–4.30pm) on the outskirts of town. In 1931 Neil McEacharn, a retired Scottish captain and passionate horticulturist, purchased the property and converted what was an unruly wooded headland into one of Europe's leading botanical gardens.

Twenty hectares (50 acres) are planted with around 20,000 different species of trees, shrubs and flowers, collected by McEacharn from five different continents, and notably Asia. A hundred gardeners were employed and the lake waters were used for irrigation. In 1952 the gardens were opened to the public and a new ferry stop, Villa Taranto, was created. McEacharn donated the complex to the state in 1938; he died here in 1964 and is buried in a mausoleum in the gardens. Eighty thousand tulips, 300 varieties of rhododendrons and a similar number of dahlias ensure colour from spring to autumn. Magnificent species of trees include cypress, sequoia, horse chestnuts from India and a splendid *Davidia Involucrata* (called the 'handkerchief tree' because of the white hanging squares it produces in spring). In the Victoria Amazonica Greenhouse the giant water lilies measure up to 2m (6.5ft) and resemble huge green trays. The flowers, which are nocturnal, only live for around 48 hours and gradually change colour from creamy white to pink and purplish red.

Gignese umbrellas

In the hills above Stresa, the village of Gignese is best known for the Museo dell'Ombrello e del Parasole (tel: 0323 89622; www.gignese.it/museo; Tue–Sun 10am–noon, 3–6pm). The museum displays 19th- and 20th-century umbrellas and parasols, and documents the life of the local umbrella-makers, some of whose descendants still make and repair umbrellas. Gignese is 8km (5 miles) from Stresa, on a road linking lakes Maggiore and Orta.

Villa Taranto, Verbania

SOUTHERN LAKE MAGGIORE

South of Laveno on the east side of the lake, the enchanting little church of **Santa Caterina del Sasso** ❹ clings to a steep cliff face above the lake (www.santacaterinadelsasso.com; Mar daily 9am–noon, 2–5pm, Apr–Oct 9am–noon, 2–6pm, Nov–Feb weekends only 9am–noon, 2–5pm). You can reach the church by taking a ferry or local boat, then climbing up 80 steps from the landing stage; alternatively, park on the square above, which is linked by a new elevator dug into the rock, or the 268-step pathway. It was thanks to a local merchant and usurer (or so it is said) that the church was founded in the 12th century. Alberto Besozzi was saved from a shipwreck in 1170 and in thanksgiving spent the rest of his life praying in a cave by the rocks where he was washed ashore. His prayers were said to have saved the area from the plague and the locals built a votive chapel to Santa Caterina. This was enlarged to a monastery in the 14th century. Beautiful

14th–19th-century fresco cycles decorate the church and the Gothic chapterhouse.

In the 11th century the twin fortresses of **Arona** and **Angera** were built to safeguard the strategic southern part of the lake. Arona's is in ruins, but the **Rocca Borromeo** (www.borromeo-turismo.it; daily late-Mar–late-Oct 9am–5.30pm) still dominates Angera. The castle became the property of the Visconti dynasty in the late 13th century and was then purchased by the Borromeo family. The oldest wing features the Sala della Giustizia (Hall of Justice), decorated with 14th-century frescoes depicting the 1277 Visconti victory over the della Torres, which brought their dynasty to power. The fortress is also home to the **Museo della Bambola**, an outstanding doll and toy museum.

The Rocca Borromeo looks across the lake to the ruined castle of **Arona**, on a rocky outcrop above the town. This was the birthplace of Saint Carlo Borromeo (1538–84), who was archbishop and cardinal of Milan and a key figure of the Counter-Reformation. Towering above the town is his huge copper statue, familiarly known as **San Carlone** (the big St Charles; www.statuasancarlo.it; mid-Mar–mid-Oct daily 9am–12.20pm, 2–6.15pm, early Mar and mid-Oct–Nov weekends only, Dec Sun only 9am–12.30pm, 2–4.30pm). You can climb right up inside the statue, and look through his eyes, though this is not to be recommended on a hot summer's day. Arona itself has a few pleasant older parts, museums and lake-view cafés, but the town gets very crowded in the summer.

NORTHERN LAKE MAGGIORE

The main resorts of the northern lake all lie on the sunny western shores. **Cannero Riviera** occupies a charming site amid subtropical flora, looking over to the picturesque ruins of the Malpaga castles. Lovely little **Cannobio**, last town before the Swiss border, has a long promenade and a delightful old quarter preserving its medieval character. In the nearby Val Cannobina, Orrido di Sant'Anna is a deep and dramatic gorge, carved out by the River Cannobino – a lovely spot for a picnic, or lunch perhaps at the restaurant Sant'Anna.

Locarno, the main resort of Swiss Lake Maggiore, is a sunny, southwest-facing town with a mild climate and flourishing parks and lakeside gardens. The heart of the town is the porticoed **Piazza Grande**, flanked by lively cafés and pizzerias where you can sit and watch the fashionable crowds go by. In summer this is the venue for open-air concerts, and in August an outdoor screen is set up for the International Film Festival (www.pardolive.ch). Southwest of the piazza, the 14th-century but much-restored Castello Visconteo is home to the Museo Archeologico, noted for its Roman remains. Up from Piazza Grande, the old town has some handsome villas, churches and the Casa Rusca art museum, with work by the French artist Jean Arp and his contemporaries.

For wonderful views of the lake and Alps take the funicular or walk up to the **Santuario della Madonna del Sasso** (daily 7.30am–noon, 3–6pm) above the resort. You can go on up from here via a glass and steel cable car to the panoramic plateau of Cardada (1,350m/4,430ft; www.cardada.ch). A 10-minute walk and a chairlift will take you higher still to Cimetta (1,671m/5,482ft), with even more staggering views.

Across the Maggia River from Locarno lies the smaller town of **Ascona**. This is another fashionable resort, and traditionally a magnet for writers and artists. Paul Klee, Hermann Hesse, Isadora Duncan and Carl Jung were among those who were lured by its charms. Klee was one of several artists in the 1920s who donated works to the **Museo di Comunale d'Arte Moderna** (Museum of Modern Art, Via Borgo 34; www.museoascona.ch; Tue–Sat 10am–noon, 2–5pm, Sun 10.30am–12.30pm). Ascona's

The main room of Rocca Borromeo di Angera

natural magnet is the lakefront promenade, with views across the water to the **Isole di Brissago**, the tiny twin islands which you can visit by boat either from Ascona or Locarno.

LAKE COMO

Celebrated since ancient times for its great natural location, Como is the most dramatic and romantic of the three great lakes. Shaped like an inverted Y, it has three branches which meet at the Punta Spartivento ('the Point that divides the Wind'), the seductive setting of the enchanting resort of Bellagio. Of the lower two branches the Ramo di Como or western branch is the most scenic, its shores studded with villas, gardens and picturesque harbours and villages. The eastern branch, known as the Lago di Lecco, is more stark and rugged and has at its southern tip the large industrial centre of Lecco.

Cannobio on Lake Maggiore

Although the lake is smaller than Maggiore and Garda, it has the longest perimeter at 170km (106 miles). It is also the deepest lake in Italy and one of the deepest in Europe (410m/1,360ft at its deepest point). In the centre, useful car-ferry services link the resorts of Menaggio, Bellagio and Cadenabbia, saving a lot of mileage and some hair-raising driving. (The road from Bellagio to Como is very narrow and precipitous.)

COMO TOWN

A large industrial centre and transport hub, **Como** ❺ may not be the obvious choice for a lakeside base. But it has a fine lakeshore setting, an historic quarter with cobbled, traffic-free streets, and some lively cafés and shops selling the famous Como silk, as well as jewellery and leather. The Piazza del Duomo in the centre is a natural magnet. The square is dominated by the lavishly sculpted facade of the **Duomo** (http://cattedrale.diocesidicomo.it; Mon–Fri 9.30am–5.30pm, Sat 10.45am–4.30pm, Sun and holidays 1–4.30pm). A fusion of Gothic and Renaissance, with a dome added in 1744, the church took some 350 years to complete. The portal is flanked by niche statues of Pliny the Elder (on the left) and Pliny the Younger (on the right) – surprising since both Plinys were pagans. The interior is full of works of art, including Renaissance tapestries hanging in the nave and paintings by Gaudenzio Ferrari (*c.*1471/81–1546) and Bernardino Luini (1480–1532), two Lombard painters influenced by Leonardo da Vinci.

Next to the Duomo is the lovely arcaded **Broletto**, the former Court of Justice, built in 1251, at the same time as the adjacent Torre del Comune (clock tower). The **Basilica di San Fedele** (daily 8am–noon, 3.30–7pm) stands on the nearby Piazza Fedele, an attractive medieval square with porticoed houses. The Lombard-Romanesque church has been much altered over the centuries and was given a new facade in the early 20th century. Originally Como's cathedral, the church was the work of the *Maestri Comacini*, medieval stonemasons of Como renowned throughout Europe for their craftsmanship. Another example

SONS OF COMO

Como's most famous sons were **Pliny the Elder** (AD 23–79), the Roman scholar who wrote the 37-volume *Historia Naturalis* (Natural History) and died during the eruption of Vesuvius in AD 79, and his nephew and adopted son, **Pliny the Younger** (AD 61–113), an author and lawyer who left a large collection of private letters offering a fascinating insight into public and private life of the times. The same Pliny is said to have owned at least two villas at Bellagio, one on the hilltop for study and reflection (possibly on the site of the current Villa Serbelloni), and another on the lakeshore for hunting and fishing.

Como's most famous scientist was **Alessandro Volta** (1745–1827), who invented the battery and after whom the volt is named. The neoclassical Volta Temple on Como's waterfront houses a collection of his instruments and inventions.

of their work is the Romanesque gem of **Sant'Abbondio** (Via Sant'Abbondio, out of the centre; daily 8am–6pm, winter 8am–4.30pm), with a remarkable cycle of mid-14th century frescoes in the apse, depicting scenes from the *Life of Christ*.

The Comaschi (citizens of Como) have been producing silk and other textiles since the 15th century and the town is the centre of Italy's silk industry. Silkworms are no longer bred here, but Chinese fibres are imported to be woven, dyed and printed. Armani, Hermès and Versace are just three of the famous designers who depend on Como for their silk. The small **Museo Didattico della Seta** (Silk Museum, Via Castelnuovo 9; www.museosetacomo.com; Tue–Fri 10am–6pm, Sat 10am–1pm) on the edge of town documents the story of Como's silk, with sections on silkworm breeding and the silk-making processes.

Locarno is in the Swiss part of Lake Maggiore

For a bird's-eye view of the town take the **Brunate funicular** ❻ which rises up the hillside east of the centre. In seven minutes you are at the hilltop village of Brunate from which there are expansive views across the lake to the Alps. Brunate can also be reached on foot from Como and makes a good starting point for hikes in the hills.

Como's highlights

Guided tours of Como's most important monuments take place every first and third Saturday of the month whatever the weather (www.visitcomo.eu; May–Sept) at the information point at Via Maestri Cumacini, flanking the Duomo.

RAMO DI COMO

The Como branch of the lake, known as the **Ramo di Como**, is best seen by boat. You can travel either by *Battello*, the regular ferry boat which stops at all the landing stages; by *Aliscafo*, the faster hydrofoil which makes fewer stops; or by excursion cruiser. Boats depart from Piazza Cavour in central Como and tickets can be purchased from kiosks on the lakefront. From Como to Bellagio the boats afford splendid views of the villages tumbling down the steep wooded hillsides and the neoclassical villas and gardens overlooking the lake.

The first main stop is **Cernobbio**, famous for the grandiose villas built here in the 16th to 18th centuries. Best known among them is the **Villa d'Este**, which since 1873 has been the most luxurious hotel on the lake (see page 137). It was built in the 16th century for Cardinal Tolomeo Gallio, Secretary of State to Pope Gregory XIII and at one time was home of Caroline of Brunswick (1768–1821), the disgraced and estranged wife of George Frederick, who later became King George IV of England.

Since becoming a hotel the villa has hosted royalty, politicians and film stars. Some of Cernobbio's splendid villas have been converted to conference or exhibition centres, such as the 19th-century Villa Erba; others are owned by wealthy businessmen or celebrities: George Clooney has a huge waterfront mansion at Laglio, a pretty lakeside village which has been used as a back-drop for his Fiat ads, and Richard Branson has a lakeside villa at Lenno. At the romantic little village of Moltrasio, 3km (2 miles) north of Cernobbio, **Villa Le Fontanelle** was the favourite haunt of the late designer Gianni Versace. The villa, whose invitees included Madonna, Elton John and a string of other celebrities, was sold to a Russian multi-millionaire after Versace's death.

Villa del Balbianello ❼ (mid-Mar–mid-Nov, Tue and Thu–Sun 10am–6pm, last entry 4.30pm) also attained celebrity status when its grounds were used for big Hollywood hits such as *Star Wars* and the Bond movie *Casino Royale*. It stands in an enchanting setting on the wooded headland south of Lenno. A private shuttle boat service runs from Lenno jetty or you can take a boat service from Como. Alternatively, on a Tuesday, Saturday or Sunday you can go by foot from Lenno (about 1km), following signs from the church square. You can wander in the gardens independently, but if you

Como Town

want to visit the villa you must take an hour-long tour.

Built as a retreat in 1787 by Cardinal Angelo Maria Durini, the villa incorporates the remains of a Franciscan convent, which you can still see at the lower level. The eccentric cardinal led a life of study and contemplation, sleeping between black sheets in a black bedroom with a coffin beside his bed to remind him of his fate. One of Durini's descendants, Count Guido Monzino, acquired the property in 1954. On his death he left the villa and contents to the FAI, the Fondo Ambiente Italiano, Italy's equivalent of the National Trust. Monzino, who led a North Pole expedition in 1971 and the first successful Italian ascent of Everest in 1973, used the villa as an international centre for the study of explorations. As well as some fine English antiques, ceramics, paintings and *objets d'art*, there is a library with hundreds of books devoted to mountaineering and polar expeditions, a map-reading room used to plan the expeditions, and a museum full of Monzino's mountaineering memorabilia. The gardens, climbing up the headland, combine magnificent oak, cypress and plane trees with immaculate lawns, romantic paths and pergolas. The climax is the open loggia at the top with glorious vistas of the lake.

Ferry trips

A ferry trip is the best way to see the lake. Coastal roads that plunge you into dimly lit tunnels and are often traffic-clogged in season do not make for relaxing driving; what's more, many of the lake's loveliest features are only visible from the water.

In the lee of the promontory the **Isola Comacina** is the only island of the lake. Tiny though it is, the settlement was fortified by the Romans and became a political and military centre in the Middle Ages, acquiring the name of Crispoli, City of Gold.

Villa d'Este in Cernobbio

The islanders supported Milan in its destruction of Como in 1128 and in retaliation Como ravaged the island in 1169, forcing them to take refuge in Varenna. The baroque Oratorio di San Giovanni and the ruins of medieval churches are all that remain. The island was bequeathed to the King of Belgium in 1914, later donated to the state and today is under the supervision of the Brera Academy of Fine Arts in Milan. A handful of artists live in cottages here. The Locanda dell'Isola Comacina dishes out an expensive lunch to tourists. Alternatively, there are plenty of peaceful spots for a picnic.

CENTRO LAGO

Grand old villas and luxuriant gardens line the lakeshores at Tremezzo. The most famous among them is **Villa Carlotta** ❽ (www.villacarlotta.it; daily late Mar–Sept 9am–6.30pm, Oct 9.30am–5pm), a vast neoclassical pile graced by over 5.6

hectares (14 acres) of gardens, and famous for its numerous varieties and huge species of azaleas and rhododendrons. The villa was built from 1690–1743 by the Clerici, a wealthy Milanese family of merchants. Most of the contents you see today were acquired by the following owner, Giambattista Sommariva. Meanwhile, his political arch rival, Duke Francesco Melzi d'Eril, constructed a beautiful villa in Bellagio, right opposite Villa Carlotta. Competition between them led to continual embellishment of both residences and gardens. In 1843 Villa Carlotta was acquired by Princess Marianna of the Netherlands, wife of Prince Albert of Prussia, who gave the villa to her daughter, Carlotta, as a wedding present – hence its present name.

The villa has a magnificent entrance with a grand stairway, gardens, balustrades and fountains. The interior, a bit of an anti-climax after the gardens, is decorated with Empire furniture and neoclassical and romantic sculpture and painting. There are works by Canova, though the much-vaunted *Cupid and Psyche* is a copy of the original which is in the Louvre.

Bellagio ❾, 'pearl of the lake', enjoys an unrivalled setting on the wooded promontory that divides the Lecco and Como arms of the lake. Walks around the cape afford sublime views of mountains in all directions, and notably north to the often snow-capped mountains along the Swiss border. The impossibly picturesque old town (or *borgo*) retains its medieval layout with porticos, cobbled alleys and stepped streets leading up from the waterside. Enticing cafés, where you can sip a cocktail and watch the ferries plying across the lake, stretch out along the waterfront. All of this of course draws boatloads of tourists throughout the season, but it is enchanting nonetheless. Ideally stay a night or two and enjoy the village after dusk when the day-trippers have departed.

On the hill behind the village are the gardens of the **Villa Serbelloni** (guided tours only, starting from the medieval tower in Piazza della Chiesa; mid-Mar–Oct Tue–Sun at 11am and 3.30pm). The villa, not to be confused with the exclusive hotel of the same name on the lakeside, belongs to the Rockefeller Foundation and is not open to the public. The steep path takes you well above the villa for sublime lake and mountain panoramas. On the south side of the village are the exotic gardens of **Villa Melzi** (www.giardinidivillamelzi.it; late Mar–Oct 9.30am–6.30pm), which spill down to the lake. The fine, if faded, neoclassical palace (closed to the public) was built for Francesco Melzi d'Eril, vice-president of Napoleon's Cisalpine Republic.

Setting off from Bellagio, passenger boats, hydrofoils and car ferries ply across the lake to Menaggio and Varenna. On the western side of the lake, **Menaggio** is larger than Bellagio and not quite as picturesque, but it has its charms and makes an excellent base for boat trips, bike tours and trekking in the hills. Large, belle-époque hotels are peacefully set along the lakeside promenade, restaurant terraces make the most of the views and there's a lively little centre with bars, small shops and a well-stocked tourist office. Golf, rock-climbing, riding, tennis, cycling, water-skiing, windsurfing and canoeing are just a few of the activities on offer – and there's a good beach and large pool at the Lido.

Villa Carlotta, Lake Como

Serious trekkers might consider the Alta Via del Lario, the route that winds from Menaggio to Gera Lario, following high ground along the Swiss border.

Manzoni's town

The commercial city of Lecco, on the southern tip of Lago di Lecco, is famous as the centrepiece of Alessandro Manzoni's masterpiece *I Promessi Sposi* (The Betrothed), published in 1827. Manzoni memorabilia can be seen at his childhood home, and locations from his novel can be identified in the town and surrounding landscape.

Varenna ⑩, across the lake, is a perfectly preserved medieval village where narrow stepped alleys lead down to a romantic lakeside walkway, shaded by porticos and arbours. In many ways this little gem is just as charming as Bellagio, but far less crowded and commercialised. Moreover, it has a handful of excellent hotels and restaurants, and two lakeside villas with gardens open to the public. **Villa Monastero** (www.villamonastero.eu; opening hours vary) is a former Cistercian convent founded in 1208 by nuns who escaped from Isola Comacina when the island was sacked by Como. Transformed into an aristocratic residence in the 17th century, the villa is now an international cultural and scientific centre, with beautiful terraced gardens spilling down to the lake, and a house museum with 14 antiques-filled rooms open to the public. Neighbouring **Villa Cipressi** (Apr–Oct 9am–6.30pm), named after its lofty cypress trees and now a hotel, also has terraced lakeside gardens open to the public. For a bird's eye view of the Bellagio peninsula, climb up steep steps or drive to the semi-ruined medieval **Castello di Vezio** (www.castellodivezio.it; early Mar–Oct, hours vary), a venue for regular falconry displays at around 3pm.

Bellagio

RAMO DI COLICO

The northern branch of the lake, called the **Ramo di Colico** or Alto Lario, has no resorts of great charm but you may like to visit the **Abbazia di Piona** (daily in season 9am–noon, 2.30–5pm). This 11th-century abbey has a pretty setting on the tip of the Olgiasca promontory enclosing the small bay of Lake Piona. The abbey was founded by Cluniac monks but is now home to Cistercians. The ruins of the Lombard Romanesque church retain early frescoes and there are beautiful Gothic/Renaissance cloisters (1252). The monks are famous for their home-made strong brews which are sold in the shop here. The abbey can be accessed by ferry in summer.

LAKE GARDA

The largest and easternmost of the lakes, Garda is bordered by three different regions: Lombardy, Trentino and the Veneto. The scenery is enormously diverse, from the fjord-like north, where the Brenta Dolomites drop sheer into the water, to the gentle hills of vineyards and olive groves, and the sea-like southern basin, fringed by beaches. Sheltered by the mountains, it enjoys an equable climate and luxuriant vegetation along its shores. Garda is the cleanest lake and the most popular for swimming, windsurfing and sailing. The lake is a favourite playground of German and Austrian tourists and in season you can expect crowded campsites and coachloads of day-trippers, particularly in the south.

THE SOUTHERN SHORES

Sirmione ⓫, Lake Garda's most famous resort, has an enticing setting on a narrow peninsula that juts 4km (2.5 miles) into the lake. The old town is heralded by the photogenic **Rocca Scaligera** (Scaligera Castle; Tue–Sat 8.30am–7.30pm, Sun 9.15am–5.45pm), accessed via a drawbridge over the fish-filled moat. The castle was built in 1259 by Mastino I della Scala, the fishtail battlements being the trademark of the della Scala family.

The narrow alleys around the castle teem with tourists throughout the season – Sirmione is just minutes away from the Milan–Venice motorway and popular with day-trippers. But beyond the castle you can escape the worst of the crowds and find pleasant lakeside terraces, beaches and a headland of olive and cypress trees. At the tip of the peninsula lies the famous **Grotte de Catullo** (www.grottedicatullo.beniculturali.it; Mar–mid-Oct Tue–Fri 8.30am–7.30pm, Sat–Sun 9.30am–6.30pm, mid-Oct–Feb Tue–Fri 8.30am–5pm, Sat–Sun 8.30am–2pm), the ruins of a vast Roman villa. The site was named after the Roman poet Catullus, but although his poems make reference to a home in Sirmione there is no evidence this was his villa. The archaeological remains – some of the most important of their kind in Italy – cover over 2 hectares (5 acres) of the promontory and are set high above the lake amid olive and cypress trees. Deciphering the various rooms on the various levels is not easy, but it is lovely just to wander around.

West of Sirmione, **Desenzano del Garda** is the largest town on the lake, and one of the most colourful and lively. An important Roman port, it retains a 3rd-century **Villa Romana** (Mar–mid-Oct

Tue–Sun 8.30am–7pm, mid-Oct–Feb Tue–Sun 8.30am–5pm and the antiquarium 9am–7pm) with remarkable floor mosaics depicting scenes of hunting and local life. The heart of the town is the picturesque **Porto Vecchio** (Old Port) flanked by cafés and the venue of a large and popular Tuesday market. Behind the port, narrow lanes lead up to the medieval castle, while along the front, the promenade is pleasant for strolling.

East of Sirmione, **Peschiera del Garda** was a medieval stronghold of the Venetian empire. The town is still dominated by the mighty bastions of its fortress, but there is not a great deal to detain you here. Nowadays, Peschiera is associated more with amusement parks than history. **Gardaland** (see page 93) is Italy's number one theme park, with 46-hectares (113 acres) of Disneyland-styled attractions (www.gardaland.it), and **Movieland Studios** (see page 93) offers film-themed attractions, shows and aquatic slides and rides (www.canevaworld.it).

Varenna perching on the shore of Lake Como

THE WESTERN SHORE

North of Desenzano the town of **Salò** ⓬ has a long history dating back to Roman times. In 1337 it became the capital of the Magnifica Patria, a community of 42 towns; during a less-fortunate episode in the town's history, it became the seat of Mussolini's puppet republic in 1943 – his last desperate attempt to reorganise

Fascism in Italy. The Art Nouveau-style Villa Simonini (now the Hotel Laurin) was the headquarters of the Italian Foreign Ministry, presided over by *Il Duce*. On a beautiful deep bay, and backed by the Monte San Bartolomeo, Salò is an appealing combination of bustling local town and elegant resort – with no hint of its ignominious past. The narrow streets and squares of the historic quarter lie behind a long lakeside promenade. The late-Gothic **Duomo** (daily 8.30am–noon, 3–6.30pm) along the waterfront, spied from afar by its distinctive bell tower, has an unfinished brick facade, with a Renaissance portal. The piazza here is the setting for summer performances of the Gasparo da Salò Festival of Music, celebrating the inventor (or perfecter) of the violin, born here in 1540.

Roman spa town

Sirmione has been a spa since Roman times. Large numbers of visitors come to its thermal establishment for treatment using the sulphurous water that emerges from a spring in the lake (www.termedisirmione.com).

Off the headland south of Salò lies the little, cypress-studded island of **Isola di Garda**. In private hands for several centuries, the island was inherited by Camillo Cavazza and the current residents are his English wife and her seven children. From April to October boats leave from Salò once a week, from Gardone Riviera twice weekly; the island can also be visited from other resorts in the lower lakes. Two-hour guided tours (occasionally given by one of the family) include the neo-Gothic villa and fine gardens, with tastings of local products such as wine and olive oil.

Just along the coast, **Gardone Riviera** ⓭ maintains much of the elegance that drew royalty and wealthy international visitors in the late 19th and early 20th centuries. The

Scaliger castle in Sirmione

Austrian Emperor and other European elite built palatial villas here and Gardone became the most fashionable resort on the lake. Among the eminent guests at the belle-époque Grand Hotel, which still stands on the waterfront, were Somerset Maugham, Nabokov and Churchill. Further along, at the Villa Fiordaliso, Mussolini stayed with his mistress Clara Petacci during the Salò Republic. This lovely Art Nouveau lakeside villa is now a hotel and restaurant where you can enjoy fine cuisine on the lake.

The biggest draw of Gardone, particularly for Italian day-trippers, is **Il Vittoriale** (www.vittoriale.it; park and gardens: daily late Mar–mid-Oct 8.30am–8pm, mid-Oct–late Mar 9am–5pm; guided tours of house Tue–Sun and War Museum Thu–Tue). This eccentric residence, set in 9 hectares (22 acres) of gardens with lake views, was home to the flamboyant poet, dramatist, soldier and socialite, Gabriele d'Annunzio (1863–1938). The memorabilia from his wartime, literary, artistic and womanising pursuits – not to mention the vast wedding cake mausoleum – are all a celebration of the man himself. Among the eccentricities are the coffin in the spare bedroom, the dark or painted windows (D'Annunzio hated daylight), an embalmed tortoise which died of overeating and the prow of the battleship, *Puglia*, wedged into the hillside.

In the early 20th century Arturo Hruska, a botanist and dentist to the last Tsar of Russia, transformed the sloping site above the town into an oasis of flora. The **Heller Garden** (www.hellergarden.com; Mar–Oct daily 9am–7pm) contains flourishing Alpine, subtropical and Mediterranean species. It's a wonderfully peaceful spot where you can wander among pretty rockeries, lush lawns, Japanese-style gardens, streams and waterfalls.

Toscalano-Maderno north of Gardone is the main embarkation point for the car ferry to Torri del Benaco. Going north, **Gargnano** is one of the main sailing centres on the lake and it is hard to find a more pleasant lakeside place to stay. Remarkably unspoilt, it has a lively little port, a promenade of orange trees, a couple of very enticing hotels (see page 139) and a gourmet restaurant serving some of the best cuisine on the lake.

The picturesque little town of **Limone sul Garda** is bypassed by the main coast road, but heaves with tourists all through the season. The rows of white stone pillars of the now-defunct lemon terraces or *limonaie* are testimony to the citrus-fruit industry

TIGNALE AND TREMÓSINE

Well worth a diversion from the shore is the panoramic route climbing up to Tignale and Tremósine, scenic plateaux of alpine meadows. (Note, though, that the narrow roads and hairpin bends are not for the faint-hearted). The 43km (27-mile) detour from the lake starts on the road 4km (2.5 miles) north of Gargnano. This snakes its way up to Tignale (555m/1,821ft), then descends before climbing up again to the Tremósine plateau – an even higher balcony commanding views of the entire lake basin. From here the main road comes down to join the lake at Limone sul Garda.

Salò at night

which made Limone rich. Trade declined in the 20th century with competition from cheaper citrus fruits grown in the hotter climate of the south. Fruit trees still flourish and market stalls brim with bottles of lemon liqueur, lemon-shaped ceramics and the freshly picked fruits. You might assume the village is named after the citrus fruit but it is more likely that it derives from the Latin *limen* or border, referring to the former frontier here between Austria and Italy.

GARDA TRENTINO

The northern tip of the lake lies in Trentino, which was under Austrian rule from 1815–1918. Set against the dramatic backdrop of Monte Brione, the main resort of **Riva del Garda** ⓮ has been luring visitors from the north since the 19th century. Today it is a thriving holiday resort, attracting a large number of German and British tourists, but managing to retain much of its former character and elegance. Strategically located between Verona and the Alps, the town was a major trading port, coveted by rival factions and variously acquired by the Veronese Scaligeri (1349), the Viscontis of Milan (1380) and the Venetian Republic (1440).

The moated **La Rocca**, dominating the waterfront and accessed over a drawbridge, is testimony to the Scaligera era. Since it was built in 1124 the castle has been remodelled several times, and under the Austrians the tower was truncated, turning the castle into a garrison. Today it is home to the Museo Alto Garda (www.museoaltogarda.it), with displays of art and archaeology and varied temporary exhibitions. Overlooking the harbour, **Piazza III Novembre** is the appealing main square, flanked by medieval Renaissance palazzi and the lofty **Torre Apponale**. The tower has variously served as a prison, a store for salt and grain, and as a look-out point during World War I.

Cafés and pizzerias along the waterfront make the most of the views, and there are parks, gardens and pebbly beaches. The waters are dotted with windsurfers and dinghies all year round – you can rent equipment and have lessons, or just take a leisurely stroll along the waterfront to admire the views. You

LIMONE'S ELIXIR OF LIFE

In the late 1980s scientists discovered that many of Limone's inhabitants had a mystery protein in their blood that declogs their arteries of fat and gives them virtual immunity to heart attacks and strokes. The chemical, called Apolipoprotein A-1 Milano (shortened to Apo A-1 Milano) has been identified in around three dozen Limonesi. The mutant gene has been passed from generation to generation – Limone was an isolated village pre-1932, only accessible by boat or by crossing the mountains, and intermarriage was common. All the carriers are descendants from the same couple who lived in Limone in the 18th century. Human trials based on Apo A-1 Milano have demonstrated proof of efficacy against cardiovascular disease in animals and humans but as yet, no drugs are commercially available; and in case you're wondering, no link has (yet) been established between the protein and Limone lemons.

can walk all the way to **Torbole** (4km/2.5miles), described by Goethe as 'a wonder of nature, an enchanting sight'. Its setting below sheer rocks and beside the River Sarca is as alluring as ever, but the village is spoilt by the main road cutting off the centre from the lake, and unless you're into rock climbing, windsurfing or sailing there is little to detain you.

THE EASTERN SHORE

Stretching 50km (31 miles) along the eastern bank of the lake, the so-called **Riviera degli Olivi** is typified by tourist development as well as olive groves and vine-clad hills. The main road, known as the **Gardesana Orientale**, hugs the shoreline and is frequently traffic-clogged in summer. The northern section, between Torbole and Malcesine, has a series of dimly lit tunnels, plunging you from dazzling bright sunlight into blackness. This tunnelled stretch is the setting of a dramatic opening car chase in the Bond film *Quantum of Solace*, climaxing in a spectacular crash.

Gargnano on Lake Garda

The resort of **Malcesine** ⓯ lies at the foot of Monte Baldo, and clusters beneath the striking Castello Scaligero. This fishing village-turned-tourist magnet is a picturesque maze of cobbled alleys, with medieval porticoes and a small port which buzzes with activity throughout the season. The **castle** (Apr–Oct daily 9.30am–7.30pm, Nov–Mar Sat–Sun and holidays 11am–4pm) has fine views of the lake from the battlements and tower, and is home to the Natural History Museum of Monte Baldo and Lake Garda.

Behind the resort the panoramic rotating cabins of a funicular whisk you up **Monte Baldo** (2,220m/7,275ft) in 10 minutes (www.funiviedelbaldo.com; late Mar–mid-Nov daily 8am–6pm). The cabins can also accommodate mountain bikes and hang gliders so you can freewheel or float back. The ridge offers some ravishing **views** and scenic walking trails. In winter the funicular takes you to the ski slopes. Malcesine is a popular hub for all sports enthusiasts: in addition to hiking, mountain biking and winter sports, there is windsurfing, kitesurfing, sailing and scuba diving on the lake, and tennis and horse riding on the shores.

Goethe at Garda

The Sala Goethe in Malcesine's castle is devoted to the German writer's drawings, notes and views on Lake Garda and the castle. While compiling his *Travels in Italy* he visited the lake in 1786 when it was under Austrian rule. The writer was sketching the castle at Malcesine when he was arrested as an Austrian spy. He was imprisoned here but soon released after convincing the authorities of his innocence.

Yet another Scaligeri castle heralds the town of **Torri del Benaco**. Views from the tower encompass almost the entire lake, from Sirmione to Limone. The castle museum is devoted to Torri's ancient way of life: boat building, fishing and olive cultivation. Modern Torri is busy with car ferries that ply across the waters to Toscolano-Maderno, but the old port has maintained its original character, and the Hotel Gardesana's café terrace, which overlooks it, is a delightful spot to watch the world go by.

Riva del Garda

In ancient times Lake Garda was called 'Benacus' (beneficent) – and it is occasionally still referred to by the Latin name. The lake took its current name from the town of **Garda** which lies below a huge rocky outcrop on the south-eastern shore. The town today is a bustling holiday resort where life focuses on a long, spacious promenade, lined by tourist cafés. Behind the waterfront the narrow alleys of the old quarter are packed with small shops, souvenirs and trattorias. **Punta San Vigilio** to the west is a delightful spot, where an ancient lane of cypress trees leads to the tip of a peaceful promontory with a little church and a 16th-century villa. On a tiny harbour the luxury hotel Locanda San Vigilio, with just 7 rooms and a lakeside restaurant, has been welcoming guests since the early 16th century. On the other side of the promontory the Baia delle Sirene (Bay of the Sirens) has a good but crowded beach and is a pretty spot to take a picnic in the shade of olive trees.

South of Garda, **Bardolino** offers plenty of opportunities for tasting the eponymous wine. Head for the excellent little **Museo del Vino** above the town (www.museodelvino.it; mid-Mar–Oct daily 9am–12.30pm, 2.30–7pm, Nov–mid-Mar 8.30am–12.30pm, 2.30–6.30pm). In the adjoining Zeni Winery (www.zeni.it) you can try the local reds, whites and rosés, and purchase bottles at very reasonable prices. In late September and early October Bardolino hosts the Festa dell'Uva (Grape Festival) where corks pop non-stop. Wines aside, Bardolino is a pleasant lakeside resort with a tree-lined promenade and a profusion of small bars and cafés and two ancient churches. At Cisano di Bardolino the **Museo dell'Olio di Oliva** (Olive Oil Museum; www.museum.it; Mon–Sat 9am–12.30pm, 2.30–7pm, Sun 9am–12.30pm) offers free tasting of local olive oil and has a little shop selling vinegars, olives, honey, pasta and pesto, as well as olive oil.

LESSER LAKES

LAKE ORTA

The westernmost of the lakes and the only one entirely in Piedmont territory, **Lake Orta** is just 14km (9 miles) long and 3km (2 miles) at its widest point. It may not sound that small but it's minute in comparison to neighbouring Maggiore, and a lot more peaceful. The highlight is **Orta San Giulio** ⓰, a perfectly preserved medieval village with mesmerising views

MONTE BALDO

The 35km (22-mile) mountain chain of Monte Baldo is famous for its profusion and variety of flora. Way back in the 16th century it became known for its rare botanical species and was visited by scholars of botany and herbalists working for European royal courts. Specialists have been exploring ever since, and now there are around 20 species which have *Baldense* as part of their official name. Among the species unique to the high ridge are *Anemone baldensis* (known as the Mount Baldo windrose) and *Veronica bonarota*.

over **Isola San Giulio**. This little island in the centre of the lake seems to float on the morning mist, and by night it's illuminated and every bit as magical.

Orta San Giulio positively oozes charm, with its cobbled, car-free alleys, ancient houses and enticing lakeside **Piazza Motta**. Nicknamed the *salotto* or drawing room, the square is overlooked by the lovely Palazzotto, the old town hall, with its loggia and faded frescoes. The little harbour is a scene of constant activity with rowing boats and water taxis plying back and forth to the island. Legend has it that San Giulio, a missionary from the Greek island of Aegina, rid the island of dragons and snakes in the 4th century and founded the basilica here. It was rebuilt in the 10th century and became a centre of pilgrimage. Though much remodelled since, the church retains its richly carved, 11th-century black-marble pulpit, frescoes from four centuries and the remains of the saint. From the basilica a peaceful cobbled path, called the Way of Silence *(Via del Silenzio)* going in one direction and the Way of Meditation *(Via della Meditazione)* in the other, circuits the island, passing a Benedictine monastery (no public access) and private villas overlooking the lake.

Malcesine

On a hill above Orta San Giulio are the 21 chapels of the **Sacro Monte** (Holy Mount; daily 9.30am–6.30pm, off season 9am–4.30pm), decorated with 17th- and 18th-century frescoes and life-size terracotta figures illustrating scenes from the life of St Francis. Even if you don't make it to all the chapels, this is a lovely location with lake views and a welcoming little restaurant (the Sacro Monte).

Traffic-free town

During the holiday season the village of Orta San Giulio is closed to traffic and, unless you are unloading at a hotel, cars must be left in the paying car park outside the centre. From here you descend to the central piazza on foot. Avoid visiting the lake on Sundays when coach-loads of tourists pour into the village.

VARESE AND ITS LAKE

Prosperous **Varese** is essentially a modern city and manufacturing centre which, given all the attractions of nearby lakes Como and Maggiore, is largely ignored by tourists. In its favour are the Art Nouveau villas, parks and gardens (it is styled *Città Giardino* or City of Gardens), sophisticated shopping and small historic centre. The Bernascone belltower rises 77m (253ft) above the centre; beside it the Basilica of San Vittore (1580–1615) was later given a neoclassical facade; and behind it the Baptistery of San Giovanni, with some remarkable 14th century frescoes, is one of the few surviving buildings from the medieval town. North of the town don't miss **Villa Panza** (Tue–Sun 10am–6pm), a beautiful 18th-century villa and gardens, which houses a major collection of modern American art that belonged to the last owner of the villa, Giuseppe Panza.

The **Sacro Monte** is a major pilgrimage site 8km (5 miles) northwest of Varese on the wooded slopes of Monte Campo dei Fiori. Along the steep Via Sacra are 14 devotional chapels with life-size terracotta figures and frescoes. From the Sanctuary of Santa Maria del Monte and its village at the top there are fine

Monte Baldo cable car

views – and even better ones if you were to carry on 5km (3 miles) to the Parco Regionale di Campo dei Fiori.

Shaped like a battered boot, **Lake Varese** is a tiny lake west of the city. This is a gentle, undramatic lake framed in rolling hills. Isolino Virginia, the tiny wooded island off the west shore, has a restaurant and the little Museum of Prehistory.

South of Varese, sitting among the industries of the Olona valley (and very poorly sign-posted), is the Renaissance gem of **Castiglione Olona** ⓱. Cardinal Branda Castiglioni (1350–1443) created this beautiful complex by bringing the new Renaissance style from Tuscany to his native village. The leading Florentine artist, Masolino, was commissioned to decorate the buildings and there are stunning frescoes depicting the *Life of the Virgin* (1428) in the collegiate church above the old quarter and the *Life of John the Baptist* (1435) in the nearby baptistery.

LAKE ISEO

Between the provinces of Bergamo and Brescia, **Lake Iseo** is comparatively tranquil and unknown. It lacks the picturesque villages of the larger lakes but has a fine setting within a ring of wooded mountains. Taking centre stage is **Monte Isola** ⓲, a large, car-free island with chestnut woods, vineyards, olive groves and a population of around 200, living in sleepy mountain and lakeside villages. A haven for day-trippers, the island offers pleasant walks, bike rides and restaurants serving fish straight out of the surrounding waters. The lake's speciality is *tinca* (tench) served with polenta, or you could be offered crayfish, trout, pike or perch, washed down perhaps with one of the local Franciacorta sparkling white wines.

Iseo is the lake's main town, and though very tourist-focused, retains a certain charm with its fine promenade and maze of narrow lanes. **Sarnico** is a popular sports centre and has an attractive old quarter of narrow streets, small squares and arcaded houses. **Lovere**, a steel-making centre with Celtic origins, dominates the northern lake. The town has a well-preserved historic quarter, an art gallery (Accademia di Belle Arti Tadini Gallery; www.accademiatadini.it) and a café-lined lakefront where the first steamer was launched on the lake in 1841. At picturesque **Pisogne**, across the water, the church of Santa Maria delle Neve is known as La Cappella Sistina dei Poveri (the Poor Man's Sistine Chapel) on account of the beautiful fresco cycle (1534) by Romanino.

From Pisogne you can drive north through the **Camonica Valley**,

Lake Lugano

Known also by the Italians as Lake Ceresio, its ancient name, the many-fingered Lake Lugano lies deep in the mountains between lakes Como and Maggiore. Just over a third of the shore belongs to Italy, the rest to the Swiss canton of Ticino. The steep wooded hills rising sheer from the water preclude development along most of its shores and lively, stylish Lugano is the only large town, with sunny lakeside promenades, café-lined piazzas, luxury shops and galleries.

Orto San Giulio

named after the Bronze-Age Camuni tribe who recorded scenes of everyday life by carving on the rocks of the valley floor. The valley is nowadays marred by industry but the rock engravings, which span several thousand years from the Ice Age to the Roman era, constitute one of the largest and finest collections of prehistoric art in Europe. The engravings are scattered all along the valley but the best examples are contained within Capo di Ponte's **Parco Nazionale delle Incisioni Rupestri** ⓳ (National Park of Rock Engravings; www.parcoincisioni.capodiponte.beniculturali.it). In this Unesco World Heritage Site, over 300,000 rock carvings are etched onto glacier-seared sandstone in an area covering 8km (5 miles). Big Rock 1, for example, is engraved with over 1,000 drawings (warriors, women, shamen and deer-hunters amongst them), which run from the Neolithic era to the Iron Age.

South of Lake Iseo lies the hilly, wine-producing region of **Franciacorta** ⓴. The **Strada del Vino Franciacorta** (www.stradadelfranciacorta.it) is an 80km (50-mile) wine route from Brescia to Lake Iseo, featuring vineyard tours and tastings. Franciacorta produces red and white wines but is best known for *spumante*, made according to Champagne methods. This is the best fizz you'll find in Italy.

LOMBARD CITIES

BERGAMO

Following the Napoleonic army on horseback in 1800, Stendhal arrived in **Bergamo** ㉑ from Milan having crossed 'the loveliest country in the world'. Today the *autostrada* and a great swathe of industry separate the cities, but Bergamo itself has seen remarkably little change over the two centuries. The modern city was constructed on the plain in the late 19th and early 20th centuries, but the **Città Alta**, the hilltop city where Stendhal stayed, is one of Italy's most alluring medieval centres.

From the **Città Bassa**, the pleasant enough but traffic-filled Lower City, a cable car takes you 100m (330ft) up the hill – and 500 years back in time. In 1428 Bergamo was swallowed up by the Venetian Republic; the great walls encircling the upper city, the fortress and the lions of St Mark all bear witness to over three and a half centuries under the sway of the Serenissima.

Piazza Vecchia

Via Gombito and Via Colleoni, lively medieval streets lined by delectable little food shops and eateries, lead from the upper cable-car terminal to the heart of old Bergamo. The enchanting **Piazza Vecchia** is a showpiece of medieval and Renaissance buildings, surrounding the beautiful Contarini fountain.

On the southern side of the square, the magnificent Venetian-Gothic **Palazzo della Ragione** (Mar daily 10am–noon, 2–6pm, Apr–Sept daily 9am–noon, 2–8pm, Sat until 11pm, Oct Sat–Sun 10am–noon, 2–6pm, Nov–Feb 10am–noon, 2–4pm) is the oldest communal palace in Italy, built in the 12th century though much remodelled. The elegant external stairway leads up to the main hall which houses a collection of fresco

Sacro Monte church fresco

panels taken from nearby churches and convents.

The glass lift in the city's bell tower, known more familiarly as the **Campanone** (www.museodellestorie.bergamo.it; Apr–Oct Tue–Fri 10am–6pm, Sat and Sun until 8pm, Nov–Mar Tue–Fri 9.30am–1pm, 2.30–6pm, Sat and Sun 9.30am–6pm), affords fine views of the town. The bell still chimes 100 times every evening at 10pm, in memory of the curfew under the Venetians. On the far side of the piazza the imposing white building is the Palazzo Nuovo, which today serves as the civic library.

Piazza del Duomo

Beyond Piazza Vecchia's loggia lies the smaller **Piazza del Duomo**, which is crammed with three major monuments. The **Cappella Colleoni** (Mar–Oct Tue–Sun 9am–12.30pm, 2–6.30pm, Nov–Feb 9am–12.30pm, 2–4.30pm) was built in 1472–6 as a mausoleum for the Venetian *condottiere* (mercenary), Bartolomeo Colleoni, who had the old sacristy of the neighbouring Santa Maria Maggiore demolished to create the space. A masterpiece of the early Lombard Renaissance, it has a multicoloured marble facade enriched by medallions, columns, sculpture and reliefs. The interior is no less opulent, decorated by Tiepolo frescoes and containing the intricately carved tomb of Colleoni, surmounted by a gold equestrian statue of the *condottiere*. The chapel also contains the tomb of his daughter, Medea, who predeceased him.

The adjoining church of **Santa Maria Maggiore** (Apr–Oct Mon–Sat 9am–12.30pm, 2.30–6pm, Sun 9am–1pm, 3–6pm, Nov–Mar Mon–Sat 9am–12.30pm, 2.30–5pm, Sun 9am–1pm, 3–6pm) has a beautiful Gothic porch adorned with statues and reliefs. The interior was reconstructed in the 16th century and has a profusion of gilt, stuccowork and paintings as well as some fine Florentine and Flemish tapestries and exquisite inlaid panels on the (roped-off) choir stalls, designed by Lorenzo Lotto. Back in the piazza, the charming octagonal **Baptistery** is a copy of the 14th-century original which used to be inside the basilica. The **Duomo** (7.30am–noon, 3–6.30pm) is the poor relation in a remarkable group of buildings, its late 19th-century facade looking somewhat sober beside that of Santa Maria Maggiore and the Cappella Colleoni.

Off Via Gombito, the Via Solata leads up to **La Rocca** (www.museodellestorie.bergamo.it; June–Sept Tue–Fri 10am–1pm, 2.30–6pm, Sat 10am–7pm, Oct–May Tue–Sun 9.30am–1pm, 2.30pm–6pm), a 14th-century fortress that was reconstructed by the Venetians. This commands fine views across the city and is home to the History Museum, dedicated to the Risorgimento. The Natural History Museum and the Archaeological Museum can be found at the **Cittadella** to the west, built as a fortress by Bernabò Visconti though much altered and restored over the centuries.

The cultural highlight of the Città Bassa is the restored **Galleria Accademia Carrara** (Piazza Giacomo Carrara 82; www.lacarrara.it; Wed–Mon 9.30am–5.30pm, times vary, see website for latest schedule), a rich collection of 15th–18th-century art, and particularly strong on the Venetian and Lombard schools. Opposite, and housed in a former convent, the GAMeC gallery of modern

Gaetano Donizetti

The composer Gaetano Donizetti, one of the great masters of bel-canto opera, was born in Bergamo in 1797. He is commemorated in the city by a street, a theatre, a memorial, a monument and the Museo Donizettiano. He was a highly successful musician but endured great tragedy in his personal life. All three of his children died at a young age and his wife succumbed to the plague. Donizetti suffered from syphilis, was institutionalised, and died in Bergamo in 1848.

and contemporary art (www.gamec.it; permanent collection Tue–Sun 10am–1pm, 3–5pm; temporary exhibitions, times vary) features some first-class temporary exhibitions.

BRESCIA

Lombardy's second city after Milan, industrial **Brescia** ㉒ lacks the charm (and the tourists) of Bergamo or Verona. You are unlikely to choose it as a base, but for those interested in art and architecture, there is an outstanding museum complex and some fine monuments reflecting the various eras of its long history. The town flourished under the Romans, who left their mark in the grid layout of the city and the Capitoline Temple. In medieval times the town became a wealthy independent commune, supplying arms and armour to Europe; but like Bergamo, it came under Venetian rule from 1426–1797.

Piazza della Loggia

Life centres on three very different squares at the centre of the city. The most appealing is the Venetian-style **Piazza della Loggia**, the loggia being the richly decorated palazzo dominating the square – today the town hall. The upper level was designed by the leading Venetian architects Palladio and Sansovino. On the south side the piazza is flanked by the Monte Vecchio di Pietà (1489) and the Monte Nuovo di Pietà (late-16th century), the old and the new pawnbrokers; on the opposite side of the square, the Torre dell'Orologio echoes St Mark's Torre dell'Orologio in Venice, with a splendid astronomical clock (1544) and two clockwork figures that strike the hour. Neighbouring **Piazza della Vittoria**, accessed via an archway, was built during the Mussolini era and couldn't be more of a contrast.

Piazza Paolo VI

The religious core of the city is **Piazza Paolo VI**, formerly the Piazza del Duomo. The square changed its name in honour of Pope Paul VI (1897–1978) who was born in Brescia. The massive **Duomo Nuovo** (New Cathedral; Mon–Sat 7.30am–noon, 4–7pm), whose huge green cupola can be seen from afar, stunts the lovely **Rotonda** (Tue–Fri 9am–noon, 3–7pm), the Duomo Vecchio or Old Cathedral. This is an unusual round Romanesque building constructed on the site of an 8th-century basilica which was destroyed by fire in 1097. The interior contains the beautifully decorated sarcophagus of Bishop Berardo Maggi (1308) in red Verona marble. The austere building with a tower to the left of the Duomo Nuovo is

Piazza Vecchia, Bergamo

Santa Maria Maggiore, Bergamo

the Broletto, the medieval town hall, today the city council offices.

Roman ruins and Santa Giulia Museo della Città

The Via dei Musei beside the Broletto takes you to the **Piazza del Foro**, the old Roman forum. Towering above it are the mighty columns of the Capitoline Temple erected in AD 73 by Emperor Vespasian. Beside the temple the **Roman Theatre** has recently been excavated (Parco Archeologico di Brescia Romana; www.bresciamusei.com; Tue–Fri 9am–5pm, Sat–Sun 10am–6pm; combined ticket for the temple and theatre). Archaeological finds from the site are housed in the nearby Santa Giulia **Museo della Città** (City Museum; Tue–Fri 9am–5pm, Sat 10am–9pm, Sun 10am–6pm), laid out in the monastery of Santa Giulia. Founded in AD 753 by the Lombard king, Desiderius, the complex was continually extended up until the Renaissance and features the Romanesque church of Santa Maria in Solario, rich in frescoes and home to the rare, bejewelled 9th-century Cross of Desiderius, and the medieval Basilica of San Salvatore whose Nun's Choir is decorated with striking early 15th-century frescoes. The museum explores some 2,000 years of the city's history (from prehistory to the Venetian era), through statuary, frescoes, mosaics, medieval graves and other works of art. From the Roman era, the highlight is the bronze life-sized statue of *The Winged Victory*, discovered in the Capitoline Temple in 1826. The Santa Giulia monastic complex was awarded Unesco World Heritage status in 2011, forming one of seven key sites chosen to represent Italy's Longobard (Lombard) civilisation from AD 568–774.

Rising above the forum is the vast 14th-century Visconti **Castello** (Tue–Fri 9am–5pm, Sat–Sun 10am–6pm), incorporating the Museum of the Risorgimento and the Museum of Ancient Arms. Due south of the Piazza del Foro, on Piazza Moretto, the **Pinacoteca Tosio-Martinengo** has a fine collection of works by Brescian Renaissance and baroque masters. The gallery is currently closed for restoration, so these are temporarily on display at the Santa Giulia Museo della Città.

CREMONA

Synonymous with Stradivarius, **Cremona** has been the centre of the violin-making industry since the 16th century. Andrea Amati created the first modern violin here in 1566 and his more famous pupil, Antonio Stradivarius, was born here in 1644. The International School of Violin Making ensures the continuation of the tradition and concerts often take place in the town. The International Festival of Stringed Instruments takes place every third October (2018, 2021 etc).

Music apart, Cremona is a provincial market town on the River Po, with a fine medieval square but not a great deal else to detain you. The city's main monuments are all grouped on the **Piazza del Comune**. The magnificent **Duomo** (Mon–Sat 8am–noon, 3.30–7pm) facade incorporates elements of the Romanesque, Gothic and Renaissance styles; inside, the nave and chancel are decorated with frescoes. The **Torrazzo**, at 113m (370ft), is the tallest bell tower in Italy – the energetic can climb 487 steps to the top for fine views over the city.

Palazzo della Loggia, Brescia

To the right of the Duomo the octagonal baptistery was built at the same time and remodelled in Renaissance style. Across from the Duomo, the red-brick Loggia dei Militii was the former headquarters of the local militia. The Palazzo dell'Arte on Piazza Marconi is home to the **Museo del Violino** (Violin Museum; www.museodelviolino.org; Tue–Sun 10am–6pm) showcasing the origins of the violin and the violin-making industry. Also on display are exquisite pieces owned by Cremona's Town Hall and the Fondazione Stauffer, including Stradivarius' Cremonese 1715. More Stradivarian memorabilia can be seen at the Museo Stradivariano within the Museu Civico Ala Ponzone (Via Ugolani Dati 4), 10 minutes' walk north of the Piazza del Comune.

MANTUA

Formerly one of the great Renaissance courts in Europe, **Mantua** (or Mantova) is nowadays a provincial town with unprepossessing outskirts and a diminished population. But it has a lovely unspoilt medieval centre concentrated around three interlinked piazzas. The vast Palazzo Ducale, the Palazzo Tè and other great architectural monuments of Mantua are testimony to the power and artistic patronage of the Gonzaga family who lorded it over the town for nearly four centuries.

Palazzo Ducale

The huge cobbled **Piazza Sordello** is dominated by the **Palazzo Ducale** (tel: 041 2411897; www.mantovaducale.beniculturali.it; Tue–Sun 8.15am–7.15pm; reservations must be made in advance to see the Camera degli Sposi, only 1,500 visitors permitted daily). The palazzo was originally built by the despotic Bonacolsi, lords of Mantua from 1272–1328. When the Gonzagas took control of the town in 1328, the palace became their fortress and home, and was extended over the centuries to become a colossal complex of over 450 rooms, with courtyards, piazzas and gardens. Although much altered, the palace still gives a vivid idea of the brilliance of the Gonzaga Court.

Among the artistic highlights are Pisanello's unfinished series of 15th-century frescoes of the *Knights of the Round Table*, 16th-century Flemish tapestries modelled on Raphael's cartoons of the *Acts of the Apostles*, Rubens' huge portrait of *The Gonzagas Adoring the Holy Trinity*, and most famous of all, the *Camera degli Sposi* (Bridal Chamber) in the Castello di San Giorgio, decorated by Mantegna's frescoes (1465–74), glorifying the Gonzaga family. A spectacular experiment of perspectival illusionism, the frescoes cover the entire room, including the architectural features. Most innovative of all is the trompe-l'oeil ceiling, with putti and ladies in waiting peering down over the foreshortened balustrade.

Piazza Broletto and Piazza delle Erbe

From Piazza Sordello an archway leads to **Piazza Broletto**, the centre of medieval public life. The red-brick Broletto is the old town hall which separates the square from Piazza delle Erbe. On the Piazza Sordello side the Torre della Gabbia was converted to a prison and has an iron cage where prisoners were put on public display.

Named after the fruit and vegetable market, the **Piazza delle Erbe** is the loveliest of Mantua's squares. It is framed on three sides by porticoes and shops, and at night you can dine out by candlelight in front of the arcades of the Palazzo della Ragione. This large 13th-century, crenellated palace hosts major art exhibitions. Below piazza level is the beautiful Romanesque (though remodelled) **Rotonda di San Lorenzo** (Mon–Fri summer 10am–1pm, 3–7pm, winter 10am–1pm, 2–6pm, Sat–Sun 10am–6pm), the oldest of Mantua's churches. The interior walls and vaults still preserve traces of Byzantine-influenced frescoes.

Basilica di Sant'Andrea

Situated on the neighbouring Piazza Mantegna, the **Basilica di Sant'Andrea** (daily 8am–noon, 3–7pm) was a major landmark in Renaissance architecture. Replacing a Romanesque church, it was designed by the great Florentine architect and theorist Leon Battista Alberti for Lodovico Il Gonzaga. Inspired by classical architecture and evoking the grandeur of ancient Rome, the basilica combines a temple front and triumphal arch. The imposing interior is laid out on a Roman basilica plan and profusely decorated. The first chapel on the left houses the tomb of the painter, Andrea Mantegna, who died in Mantua in 1506.

Sons of Mantua

Mantua's most famous sons are the poet Virgil, whose statue you can see in a niche on Palazzo Broletto, and Andrea Mantegna, who was court painter to the Gonzagas and produced the famous Camera degli Sposi in the Palazzo Ducale.

Palazzo Tè

A bus ride or 20-minute walk from the centre will bring you to **Palazzo Tè** (www.palazzote.it; Tue–Sun 9am–6.30pm, Mon 1–6.30pm). This exuberant villa was built and decorated in the mannerist style by the architect and painter Giulio Romano (1499–1546) for the pleasure-loving Federico II Gonzaga and his mistress, Isabella Boschetti. Fantastic frescoes adorn the rooms, ranging from the life-size horses of the Gonzagas to the erotic murals of the Sala di Amore e Psyche (Cupid and Psyche Room). The tour de force is the Sala dei Giganti (Room of the Giants) depicting the victory of Jupiter over the rebellious Titans. The entire room, including the vaulted ceiling, is frescoed to give an illusionistic effect, with rocks tumbling down onto the Titans (and seemingly the spectators too).

The Capitoline Temple, Brescia

VERONA

Verona ㉓ is a city of superlatives: the largest and most enticing city in the Veneto after Venice, boasting the world's third-largest Roman amphitheatre, some of the finest piazzas and monuments in northern Italy, along with the grandest open-air opera. Above all, however, Verona is celebrated for Shakespearean tales of young love. Crowds from all corners of the world come to pay respects to the so-called Casa di Giulietta (Juliet's House) and the famous marble balcony.

Strategically placed on the River Adige at a crossing of major trade routes, the town flourished under Roman rule, but it was

Mantua reflections

under the hugely powerful and frequently tyrannical Scaligeri (or della Scala) dynasty (1260–1387) that the city reached its zenith. The Visconti from Milan had a brief spell as lords of Verona; but from 1405 the city came under the sway of the Venetians, who ruled here until the French invasion of 1796.

PIAZZA BRÀ AND THE ARENA

The natural tourist magnet is the spacious **Piazza Brà** Ⓐ, dominated by the **Arena** Ⓑ (Tue–Sun 8.30am–7.30pm, Mon 1.30–7.30pm, off season until 5pm, during opera festival until 4pm). Built in the 1st century AD, this is the world's third-largest Roman amphitheatre after the Colosseum in Rome and the Campano Amphitheatre at Capua in Campania. Elliptical in form, it measures 73m x 44m and has 44 marble tiers, seating 20,000. The outer wall was damaged by a series of earthquakes in the 12th century; otherwise it is remarkably well-preserved. In Roman times it was the scene of gladiatorial combat, mock battles and games; today it is the stage for the world-famous Verona opera performances. On the west side of the square, the gently curving Listone is lined by open-air cafés, pizzerias and restaurants, a popular rendezvous and favourite spot to watch the leisurely *passeggiata* (evening stroll) and street-theatre performers.

PIAZZA DELLE ERBE

From the Listone, the elegant, shop-lined Via Mazzini brings you into bustling **Piazza delle Erbe** **C**, the heart of Verona and formerly the Roman forum. The market nowadays is more a source of snacks and souvenirs than herbs or fresh produce, but it is still an appealing piazza with its white canopies, handsome palazzi, marble fountain and monuments. Finest of the palaces is the baroque Palazzo Maffei, surmounted by six statues of Roman gods and flanked by the Gardello Tower (1370). On the west side is the over-restored crenellated Casa dei Mercanti (14th century); across the square the much-restored Casa Mazzanti was built for the Scaligeri family and decorated with 16th-century frescoes. On the same side is the Domus Nova (1659) and the Palazzo della Ragione (Palace of Justice).

PIAZZA DEI SIGNORI AND ARCHE SCALIGERE

Linking Piazza dei Signori with Piazza delle Erbe is the Arco della Costa, 'arch of the rib' – the rib referring to the whalebone hanging below the arch, which – according to legend – will fall on the first honest person to pass underneath. Centre of civic life until the 16th century, the **Piazza dei Signori** **D** is a far more formal square than Piazza delle Erbe, reminiscent of a stage set from a Shakespeare play. The trio of civic buildings are the **Palazzo della Ragione** **E**, the Palazzo del Governo, and – most elegant of all – the Venetian Renaissance **Loggia del Consiglio**, topped by five statues of famous Romans. The Palazzo della Ragione, with a pretty courtyard and Gothic stairway, underwent major restoration and has opened as a centre for exhibitions of art. For panoramic views take the elevator or steps up the Torre dei Lamberti (http://torredeilamberti.it; Mon–Fri 10am–6pm, Sat–Sun 11am–7pm, last entry 45 minutes before, ticket includes Modern Art Gallery entry), the watchtower of the medieval palace.

Piazza Broletto, Mantua

Beyond the arch at the north end of the square lies the little Romanesque church of Santa Maria Antica and the **Arche Scaligere**, the extraordinary Gothic mausoleums of the Scaligeri family. These are so lofty it is difficult to see any detail – though you can spot the Scaligeri symbol of the five-rung ladder *(scala)* on the palisade that surrounds them. The most conspicuous is the equestrian tomb of Cangrande ('The Big Dog') which is a copy of the original, now in Verona's Castelvecchio.

LA CASA DI GIULIETTA

There is no evidence that the **Casa di Giulietta** F was Juliet's house – or even that Romeo and Juliet existed. The medieval dwelling was acquired by the city of Verona in 1907 and the famous balcony (which is far too high anyway for Romeo to have climbed) was added in 1935. Nevertheless, Shakespeare fans and romantics flock here to gaze at the tiny courtyard and marble balcony. The walls have been cleaned of graffiti and Juliet pilgrims are now requested to leave their love messages on the board inside the entrance arcade, in the mailbox or on the Juliet website.

The bronze statue of Juliet is a focus of attention, particularly the gleaming right breast (rubbing it is said to bring you luck in love). The house interior (Tue–Sun 8.30am–7.30pm, Mon 1.30–7.30pm, last admission daily 6.45pm) feels far from medieval but enables visitors to pose on the balcony. Romeo and Juliet Verona tours also include 'Juliet's Tomb' in a Franciscan monastery 800m (775 yards) south of Piazza Brà. Fans from around the world get married here in civil ceremonies.

CHURCHES AND ROMAN THEATRE

South of the Casa di Giulietta is **San Fermo Maggiore** ❻ (www.chieseverona.it; Mar–Oct Mon–Sat 10am–6pm, Sun 1–6pm, Nov–Feb Mon–Sat 10am–1pm, 1.30–5pm, Sun 1–5pm), a beautiful Romanesque church which was reconstructed in the 14th century.

VISITING VERONA

Verona may be steeped in history, but the heart of the city is very much alive, especially during the opera season. Tourists mainly visit on fleeting half-day tours, but this is a city which merits at least a one-night stay to take in the wealth of sights – and ideally the opera too. Nearly all of the city's attractions are found in the historic quarter, and can easily be covered on foot. The streets of the centre are largely traffic-free and the city lends itself to strolling. Sightseers can take advantage of the VeronaCard, valid for one or two days which allows unlimited travel on city buses and admissions to museums, monuments and churches.

You don't have to be an opera buff to enjoy a performance in Verona's arena. The open-air experience in one of the world's great Roman amphitheatres is an unforgettable one – even if you can't understand a word. The mood is festive and fun rather than formal. You can take your own food (alcohol is not allowed but there are vendors selling wine). The programme features favourite operas, typically *Aida*, *Carmen* and *Tosca*, and the performances are lavish affairs (see page 86).

The interior has a wealth of frescoes and a magnificent Gothic ship's-keel roof. Don't miss the Romanesque Chiesa Inferiore (Lower Church) over which the main church was built and which today serves as a crypt.

Northeast of Piazza dei Signori is **Sant'Anastasia** (same hours as San Fermo), the largest church in Verona, with a soaring Gothic interior and vast red marble pillars dividing the aisles. Among the many frescoes is Pisanello's *St George and the Princess* (1433–8) above the arch of the Pellegrini Chapel to the right of the altar. To the northwest, near the river, is the Romanesque/Gothic **Duomo** (Mar–Oct Mon–Sat 10am–5.30pm, Sun 1.30–5.30pm, Nov–Feb Mon–Sat 10am–1pm, 1.30–5pm; Sun 1.30–5pm), which has a finely carved portal and, inside, an *Assumption* (1530) by Titian (first chapel to the left of the main entrance). More charming than the actual Duomo is the ancient little San Giovanni in Fonte, originally the baptistery, and the Church of St Elena, both accessed through the door below the Duomo's organ.

Across the river lie the ruins of the **Roman Theatre** (Tue–Sun 8.30am–7.30pm, Mon 1.30–7.30pm). With beautiful views of the city, this provides a fine setting in summer for the Shakespeare Festival, concerts, ballet and jazz (see page 87). From here you can take a lift up to the monastery where exhibits from the small Archaeological Museum are displayed.

Letters to Juliet

Juliet's Club was set up to sustain the myth of Romeo and Juliet and the romantic image of Verona. Thousands of unsolicited letters arrive each year, from all over the world, addressed to the Shakespearean heroine. These are all read and each one is answered by one of the many volunteer Juliet secretaries. If you want to add to the fan mail, visit www.julietclub.com.

CASTELVECCHIO AND SAN ZENO MAGGIORE

Verona's Arena

In the 1350s, Cangrande II della Scala built the **Castelvecchio** Ⓗ beside the Adige River as a fortress and residence. The triple-arched Ponte Scaligeri (rebuilt after destruction in World War II) was constructed across the river here as a private bridge and an escape route in the event of enemy attacks or local rebellions. The building has been beautifully converted to the **Museo di Castelvecchio** (Tue–Sun 8.30am–7.30pm, Mon 1.30–7.30pm). The collection includes some fine examples of medieval sculpture as well as paintings by Carpaccio, the Bellinis, Mantegna, Tiepolo and other Venetian masters.

A walk westwards along the river bank from Castelvecchio will take you in the direction of **Basilica di San Zeno Maggiore** Ⓘ (Mar–Oct Mon–Sat 8.30am–6pm, Sun 12.30–6pm, Nov–Feb Mon–Sat 10am–1pm, 1.30–5pm, Sun 12.30–5pm), arguably the finest Romanesque church in northern Italy. San Zeno, a 4th-century saint, built the original church on this site, and his tomb lies in the crypt along with those of other saints and bishops. The facade is beautifully proportioned and features a rose window representing the wheel of fortune, a main portal with marble bas-reliefs and wooden doors with 48 superb bronze panels of biblical scenes. The interior is spacious and simple, with Andrea Mantegna's exquisite triptych, *Madonna and Saints* (1459) on the high altar.

Windsurfing on Lake Garda

WHAT TO DO

SPORTS AND OUTDOOR ACTIVITIES

The lakes are a sporting paradise. You can choose from a huge range of aquatic sports, trekking in the hinterland, mountain biking, horse riding, golf or – for the more adventurous – paragliding, hang-gliding and canyoning.

WATERSPORTS

Lake Garda is a haven for sailors and windsurfers, particularly in the north where the lake narrows and the winds create ideal conditions all year round; Sirmione in the south is another good spot for windsurfing. The resorts of Riva del Garda and Torbole have numerous watersports schools with gear to rent and tuition for all levels. Gargnano hosts the annual Centomiglia sailing regatta in early September, with over 300 boats racing around the lake. Lake Como has sailing, windsurfing and water-skiing; you can hire motorboats from Como, and some main resorts such as Menaggio on Lake Como have beaches, pools and water sports. Bellagio has a lido, complete with beach, bathing area, sunbeds, cocktail bar, restaurant and a taxi shuttle service to and from Cadenabbia.

Swimming. There are a number of great places to swim in the lakes, particularly Lake Garda, which has the cleanest and warmest waters of the three main lakes. Some resorts provide lidos with beaches, pools, water sports and activities for children; others have just a narrow strip of shingle. The waters around the town of Como are polluted but as you go further north the lake becomes much cleaner.

HIKING, CLIMBING AND CABLE CARS

Trekkers are increasingly attracted by the quiet routes and breathtaking views above the lakes. The ridges and Alpine foothills offer some wonderful walking, from easy lake or woodland trails to strenuous climbs in the mountains. The Club Alpino Italiano (www.cai.it) organises guided tours and runs refuges along the mountain itineraries. The best months for walks in the Alps are May to October.

For those who want the views without the hike, there are some spectacular cable-car/funicular trips including Malcesine to Monte Baldo, Stresa to Monte Mottarone and Como to Brunate. Beware however, that the summer haze frequently restricts what should be amazing views.

As well as the views, the Monte Baldo ridge on Lake Garda, accessed from Malcesine by funicular, offers opportunities for mountaineering, hang-gliding, free climbing and canyoning, from amateur to competitive level. Further north around Torbole and Riva del Garda free climbers hang above the lake and further north the town of Arco hosted the IFSC climbing and paraclimbing world championships in 2011 and climbing youth championships in 2015. Above Lake Como the peaks of the Grigna and Resogone are for serious hikers, and there is free climbing at Lecco.

CYCLING AND MOUNTAIN BIKING

Cycling is a serious pursuit in the region and there is even a museum devoted to it on the Madonna del Ghisallo hilltop south of Bellagio (www.museodelghisallo.it). Mountain biking is particularly popular, especially on Monte Baldo and the northern end of Lake Garda, the hills and mountains around Lake Como and Mottarone above Stresa on Lake Maggiore. In summer the ski slopes make natural trails for mountain biking, cycling and hiking. Mountain-biking itineraries are supplied by local tourist offices, bikes and helmets can be hired and guides are also available.

GOLF

Golf courses are dotted around the region, many of them with wonderful views of the lakes and Alps. Among the most prestigious courses are the Villa d'Este Golf Club (www.golfvilladeste.com) near Montorfano, southeast of Como, and the Franciacorta Golf Club.

Mountain biking

SPECTATOR SPORTS

The Italian Grand Prix takes place in September at Monza, 15km (9 miles) northeast of Milan. Soccer, as in the rest of Italy, is hugely popular: the rival Milan clubs, AC Milan and Inter play at the San Siro Stadium, Via Piccolomini 5, 5.5km (3.5 miles) from the centre of Milan. Tickets can be booked through the AC and Inter websites on www.acmilan.com and www.inter.it.

OTHER SPORTS

Lombardy has 110 peaks exceeding 3,000m (9,840ft) and 600km (373 miles) of ski slopes. In the winter months it's possible to ski and snowboard at Monte Baldo (Lake Garda), Mottarone (Lake Maggiore), the Grigna mountains above Lecco (Lake Como) and the resorts above Bergamo and Brescia, but you can't always guarantee the snow. For information on ski resorts, consult www.skiinfo.it. There are plenty of opportunities for horse riding in the hills and valleys and along the ridges. Equestrian centres offer lessons for all standards, as well as one- or two-day horse-riding tours.

Waiting for the Opera to start at Verona's arena

ENTERTAINMENT

Most of the towns and villages on the lakes are peaceful places where visitors are content with a stroll and a drink or two in a lakeside bar or café. Lake Garda generally attracts a younger crowd and is the liveliest of the lakes, particularly Desenzano in the south, with bars, live music and around half a dozen nightclubs in and around the resort. Bardolino, on the other side of the lake, is quite a lively spot with plenty of bars open late as well as a couple of discos.

The larger towns in the region have bars with occasional live music, a jazz club or two, wine bars and discos which are often on the town outskirts. **Brescia**, a university city, is lively after dark especially on weekends. You can wine and dine at one of the many restaurants and wine bars in the piazzas and streets of the old town, enjoy concerts and opera at the Teatro Grande, live it up at late-night bars or just wander up to the castle to enjoy the views and an *aperitivo* on a café terrace.

Verona is famous for its Arena where opera extravaganzas are staged from late June to the end of August. Performances alternate, so that during one month you have a choice of at least four operas. Book well in advance – you can do so online at www.arena.it or by telephoning the call centre on (+39) 045 8005151. The Arena's website gives the full programme and a detailed seating plan. Seats range from the most expensive stalls (€200) to the unreserved stone steps up in the gods (€20–25). Hotels in the city get booked up well in advance for this period, so it is well worth checking that accommodation is available before reserving seats (www.veronabooking.com). An alternative is to stay on the Verona side of Lake Garda and either drive or take a late public bus back from Verona to the lake.

At the same time as the operas, Verona's Roman Theatre stages the open-air **Shakespeare Festival** (with occasional performances in English), as well as concerts, ballet and jazz performances. For details and to book online, visit www.estateteatraleveronese.it. Last-minute tickets are sold shortly before the performances. Free concerts are held regularly in the Piazza dei Signori during the summer months. Verona is also a great place for eating out, with numerous restaurants ranging from simple little trattorias to temples of gastronomy. The Listone on Piazza Bra, overlooking the Arena, is a lovely spot either for a pre- or post-prandial drink, *gelato* or full meal.

Stresa's **Settimane Musicali di Stresa** (www.stresafestival.eu) is an annual festival of classical concerts, performed by internationally renowned artists. The venues are churches, castles and villas located around Lake Maggiore and Lake Orta, and on the Borromeo Islands.

APERITIVI

In Italian towns the pre-prandial *aperitivo*, from around 6–9pm, is a way of life. The price of the drink may seem steep, but snacks, canapés and sometimes a whole buffet is included in the price and can provide a cheap alternative to dinner in a restaurant.

Aperitifs at The Brothers Cafe

Happy hour (two drinks for the price of one) is usually 7–9pm or 8–10pm. Cafés and bars offer a remarkable range of beverages: Prosecco or *spumante* (Italian sparkling wine, which you can have by the glass), *pirlo* (white wine with Campari or Aperol), Negroni (Campari with vermouth and gin) and a long list of liqueurs and other cocktails. An *enoteca* or wine bar will have a huge list of vintage and non-vintage bottles, with snacks or sometimes main courses to go with them.

SHOPPING

Northern Italians demand style and elegance and this is reflected in the shops in cities such as Brescia, Bergamo and Verona. Lakeside villages and resorts are more limited but the larger among them have some stylish fashions, and plenty of shops selling silk and leather, gourmet food, olive oil and wine.

FASHIONS

Serious fashion followers will head for nearby **Milan**, trend-setting capital of Italy (for details see *Berlitz Pocket Guide Milan*). But there are other cities in the region offering a stylish selection of fashions, leather and jewellery. **Verona** is an appealing place to shop, especially the traffic-free Via Mazzini in the centre with its designer (and other) boutiques and **Bellagio** and **Menaggio** have some stylish shoe and gift shops. **Brescia** is another good shopping city, with well-known designer stores, jewellery shops, antiques and art galleries. The streets of **Bergamo**'s Città Bassa (Lower Town), especially Il Sentierone and Via XX Settembre, offer a wide choice of fashions, leather goods, especially high quality shoes and jewellery.

Como is famous for high-quality silk, with shops offering dazzling displays of silk scarves, ties and shawls. The tourist office has a list of silk factory outlets in the area where you can get 40–70 percent discounts on silk prints, scarves, ties, and shirts which are produced for the top fashion designers.

SHOPPING OUTLETS

For elegant silk-lined jackets, hand-painted square scarves, cushions, silk stoles and blouses at 30–50 percent discount head to the outlet of Frey Emporio della Seta (www.frey.it) at Via Risorgimento 49 in Fino Mornasco south of Como. Close to Brescia the functional but well-designed **Franciacorta Outlet Village** in Rodengo Saiano (7km/4.5 miles west of Brescia, Ospitaletto exit off the A4 motorway; www.franciacortaoutlet.it) has 150 stores selling clothing, shoes, accessories, cosmetics, household items, linens and electrical goods. At the **Foxtown Outlet** (www.foxtown.ch) in the Swiss village of Mendrisio, 15km (6 miles) northeast of Como, you can snap up bargains from top brands such as Gucci, Versace, D&G and Prada. Armani fans should head for its outlet at Via Provinciale per Bregnano 13, Vertemate (south of Como) which has some great bargains in its three-storeyed warehouse.

MARKETS

Watch out for the local weekly or fortnightly markets in the larger towns where you can pick up anything from fashions

Flowers for sale in Garda's Saturday market

and handbags to whole hams and cheeses. The largest market in the region is at **Luino** on Lake Maggiore's eastern shore, which claims to be the biggest weekly market in Europe. There are some 350 stalls, attracting bargain hunters from Switzerland, Austria and Germany – as well as Italy. Some of the main towns host monthly antiques markets where you can browse among handicrafts, worthless junk or genuine antiques. **Brescia**'s Mercatino dell'Antiquariato, held in the Piazza della Vittoria on the second weekend of the month, is one of the best. Look out for the work of goldsmiths, engravers and wrought-iron artisans in Bergamo and Brescia, and ceramicists around Mantua. Local tourist offices can supply you with details of markets and any food and wine fairs that are coming to the region. Bargaining at any of the markets is always worth a try, however limited your Italian.

FOOD AND WINE

Lakeside villages and resorts teem with tiny delis selling everything from home-cured hams, speciality risotto rice, herbs and honey to local wines, grappa and liqueurs. The best olive oil in the region is made around Lake Garda, a pale aromatic oil. The panettone Christmas cake, made with raisins and candied orange and lemon zest, is a Milanese speciality; nowadays it's sold all year round throughout Italy and abroad.

Cremona is known for *torrone*, Italy's version of nougat, and *mostardo di Cremona*, which is pickled fruits in mustard oil. Local wines are often a good buy, whether it's the reds from Bardolino (Lake Garda) or Valtellina (near Lake Como), the sparkling whites from Franciacorta (Lake Iseo) or the Valcalepio wines from the province of Bergamo. Tourist offices can supply details of wine tours, estates and cellars.

Bergamo's medieval Città Alta (Upper City) has delis to die for, with counters along the Via Gombito laden with wonderful arrays of prosciutto, pasta and regional wines. Try the Salumeria Angelo Mangili at Via Gombito 8, a long-established little deli packed with fresh pasta, whole hams and cheeses. In the Città Bassa (Lower Town) Agripromo (Via Borgo Palazzo 128) specialises in authentic local produce such as salami, polenta della Bergamasca, olive oil and Valcalepio wines. A

TORRONE FROM CREMONA

Legend has it that at their sumptuous wedding feast in 1441 Bianca Maria Visconti and Francesco Sforza were presented with a magnificent dessert in the shape of Cremona's belltower (known as the Torrione). Made of egg whites, honey and nuts, it was named after the tower and presented to courts throughout Europe. Modern *torrone* is a popular confectionary like nougat, usually made industrially and sold throughout Italy and beyond. A few artisans do however remain faithful to the old recipes. Cremona still clings to the *torrone* culture – and every October hosts a *torrone* festival.

Torrone, a local speciality

regular bus service links both the upper and lower town of Bergamo with Orio del Serio airport just 5km (3 miles) away, making it ideal for last-minute shopping. If you don't make it to the town you can always stock up at the **OrioCenter** across the road from the airport, which is one of Europe's largest shopping centres (www.oriocenter.it).

CHILDREN'S LAKES

Although the lakes cater more for adults than children, there is no shortage of activities for youngsters. Along with ferry and cable-car rides there are pedaloes, rowing boats and kayaks to hire, parks and medieval castles to visit, and on Lake Garda, the largest theme park in Italy. All the lakes have watersports tuition available and some resorts have sandy or pebble beaches or lidos equipped with pools. Theme parks apart, the most exciting rides are the **Monte Baldo cable car** (www.funiviedelbaldo.com), where the rotating panoramic pods ascend Monte Baldo from Malcesine on Lake Garda, and the **Alpyland Coaster** (www.alpyland.com), above Lake Maggiore, which enables you to control a two-man bob sleigh down Monte Mottarone at speeds of up to 40kmph (25mph).

Peschiera on Lake Garda is a children's paradise – not the town itself, but the stretch of shoreline to the north which has no fewer than three theme parks. Italy's number-one theme park, **Gardaland** (at Castelnuovo 5km/3 miles north of Peschiera; tel: 045 6449777; www.gardaland.it; daily 10am–6pm, with exceptions). The theme park boasts 40 attractions and 40 shows, plus the Sea Life aquarium (www.sealifeeurope.com). Laser shows and fireworks add to the attractions on summer evenings. Be prepared for very long queues in summer. Tickets can be booked online. Just to the north, **Movieland** (www.movieland.it) offers more thrilling rides, film-themed shows with stage sets and special effects, and a fun-filled Acqua water park with a variety of rides and slides, a white-sand beach and an adventure island. **Acquasplash Franciacorta** (at Corte Franca, near Lake Iseo) offers plenty of aquatic activity with swimming pools, slides and chutes.

LAKE TRIPS BY BOAT

Hopping on a ferry is a great way of seeing the lakes. The first steamboats were launched in 1826; nowadays you can travel on hydrofoils *(aliscafi)*, excursion cruisers, car ferries *(traghetti)* as well as the reasonably priced *battelli* (passenger ferryboats) which link up the towns and villages. Timetables are widely available from ticket offices and tourist information offices. Ferries run throughout the year, though services are less frequent off-season.

Drinks and snacks are usually available on board, and some ferries operating longer routes offer a three-course set lunch. On lakes Maggiore, Como and Garda, ferries are operated by Navigazione Laghi (visit www.navlaghi.it for maps and timetables). On the larger lakes, no single pass covers the entire lake, but the area is divided into zones for which you can purchase a 24-hour pass.

Parco della Villa Pallavicino at Stresa on Lake Maggiore is a popular spot for youngsters, with 40 different species of animals and birds, many of them roaming free in the park, and a well-equipped playground. In summer a little electric train links the park with central Stresa. On the other side of the lake **Rocca Borromeo** is one of the region's best-preserved castles, and home to a doll museum. Lake Garda has several medieval castles.

Budding gladiators can let their imaginations run wild in Verona's beautifully preserved **Roman Arena**, and older children might enjoy one of the opera extravaganzas (this is not formal opera – you can sit on the steps up in the gods and take a picnic). For other ideas to keep kids amused in Verona visit www.veronaforkids.it.

Teacups at Gardaland

CALENDAR OF EVENTS

There are numerous annual events around the lakes, from Verona's world-famous operas and Milan's fashion fairs to low-key food and wine festivals and local village events. Information is available from local tourist offices. The following is a selection of the highlights:

February/March: Carnival in Verona, Lecco and other towns and villages; parades, floats, music and dancing.

March: Stresa's spring to autumn *Settimane Musicali* begins.

Early April: Celebrations at Pontida, Bergamo, to mark the 1176 defeat of Barbarossa by the Lombard League.

Easter: Parade of symbolic floats at Bormio near Sondrio and costumed parade at Schivenoglia, Mantova.

Last Sunday of May: Legnano's *Sagra del Carroccio*: medieval pageant and *palio* contest commemorating the Lombard League's 1176 victory.

June: International piano festival, Bergamo. Festival of San Giovanni Battista, 24 June, Isola Comacina, Lake Como; mass in the ruins of the basilica, candlelit boat procession and fireworks.

Late June–August: Verona's opera season at the Arena (www.arena.it) and the Shakespeare Festival at the Teatro Romano, Verona, with English-language performances by the Royal Shakespeare Company; also jazz, ballet and modern-dance performances (www.estateteatraleveronese.it).

July: International Sailing Regatta at Gargnano, Lake Garda. Third week: Lago Maggiore Jazz, performances at Stresa, Angera and other towns on Lake Maggiore, attracting big names in the world of jazz.

August: Illuminated boat race followed by fireworks at Laveno Mombello, near Varese. Ten-day Film Festival at Locarno, Lake Maggiore.

August–September: *Palio Baradello* at Como, celebrating the victory of Barbarossa over Milan.

September: Italian Grand Prix at Monza (first week). Music Festival in Ascona, Lake Maggiore. Como's international music festival (Sept–Nov). *Mostro Autunno Pavese*, gastronomic festival in Pavia. *Festa dell'Uva* (Grape Festival) on the last weekend of the month, Bardolino, Lake Garda. Franciacorta wine and food festival. Firework display, Sirmione, Lake Garda.

EATING OUT

Eating out is one of the great pleasures of a holiday in the lakes. Many of the restaurants enjoy seductive lakeside settings, and offer a wide choice of appetising dishes from smoked cured hams and seasoned sausages to creamy risottos, flavoursome pastas and fish fresh from the lake. Each region has its specialities: from Brescia comes *casonsèi*, giant ravioli stuffed with parmesan, spinach and eggs; from Lake Iseo the highly prized baked *tinca* or tench, served with polenta; from Mantua, *tortelli di zucca*, delicate egg pasta enveloping pureed pumpkin; from Milan the famous *risotto alla milanese*, coloured and flavoured with saffron.

Rice, rather than pasta, is the mainstay of the local diet, grown on the vast paddy fields around the Po and in the Veneto. Meat and dairy products are abundant, with butter, rather than olive oil, used in Lombard cuisine. Cheeses, from the Parmesan-like *grana* to the creamy cows' milk cheeses, appear on every menu, either enriching pastas and risottos or served on a platter with fresh bread and olive oil. Fresh herbs and vegetables, such as *porcini* mushrooms, artichokes, red chicory and asparagus, are key ingredients, grown in abundance and used with fish, meat, risotto and pasta.

WHERE TO EAT

There are dozens of casual, family-run trattorias serving authentic local dishes, as well as more classy and elegant places catering for gourmets. Although traditionally a **ristorante** is smarter, more professional and expensive than a **trattoria**, the difference between the two nowadays is negligible. An **osteria**, traditionally a tavern or inn serving wine and pasta, can be any type of restaurant, from traditional to hip. The ubiquitous **pizzeria** usually offers a wide-ranging menu including many types of pasta, meat dishes and even fish, as well as pizzas. The best pizzas come bubbling hot from a wood-fired brick oven (in small towns only available in the evening), the worst are thick-based squares with a thin layer of tomato and cheese topping, served in cafés during the day. *Pizza al taglio*, sold by the slice with a variety of toppings, is the most popular Italian takeaway food item.

Alfresco dining overlooking Lake Como

An **enoteca** or wine bar will have a wide selection of fine wines with a platter of cheese or cold meats to accompany them. A **tavola calda** is a self-service or takeaway with hot meals such as pasta, risottos, meat and vegetable dishes. For a quick bite, go to a **bar** or **café** where you can find a selection of rolls with savoury fillings and *tramezzini* (crustless, generously filled sandwiches). Standing at the bar *(al banco)* is always a lot cheaper than sitting at a table with waiter service.

In the larger resorts a whole string of waterside cafés and pizzerias will be vying for your trade, some advertising a *menu turistico* in several languages. Often the better-value places are in side streets, away from the waterfront or on the edge of town, though it's hard to resist the lakefront views.

WHAT TO EAT

As in the rest of Italy, restaurants (as opposed to pizzerias) offer four courses: *antipasto* (the hors d'oeuvre), *primo* (the first course, which is pasta, risotto or soup), *secondo* (the second course, i.e. fish or meat) and finally the *dolce* (dessert). Traditionally you were expected to have at least three courses; now, in most establishments, it's quite acceptable to opt, say, for an *antipasto* followed by a pasta dish, or perhaps a pasta dish followed by a dessert.

Antipasti

The selection of hors d'oeuvres will typically include *antipasto di pesce*, which is likely to be marinated freshwater fish such as *persico* (perch), *tinca* (tench) or *lavarello* (a lake white fish) and an *antipasto di carne*, a selection of cold meats such as thinly sliced *prosciutto crudo* (cured ham), mountain hams, salami, seasoned sausages, smoked beef, *bresaola* (dried salted beef) or, in Trentino, *Speck* (cured smoked ham).

Fresh gilt-head prepared with citrus fruits and herbs

The cold cuts will come with bread, extra-virgin olive oil (Lake Garda produces the best) and perhaps with *mostarda de Cremona*, which is fruit pickled in a mustard sauce. Around Lake Como, restaurant menus may feature *missoltini* or *missultitt*, sun-dried salted shad which is lightly grilled and served with oil and vinegar.

Set menus

Set menus vary from a basic two- or three-course meal, usually with a choice of meat or fish, to a seven-course blow-out *menu degustazione*, giving you the chance to try several house specialities. All set menus include service and cover charge; some also throw in house wine, mineral water and coffee.

Il Primo

Rice is prepared in dozens of different ways, enriched with fish, seafood, meat and vegetables. The ingredients will vary according to the seasons. The most famous rice dish of the region is *risotto alla milanese*, made with short-grain Arborio rice, stock, beef marrow, onions, saffron and Parmesan cheese.

Other popular combinations are *risotto ai funghi*, with mushrooms (often *porcini* or wild mushrooms); *risotto alla pescatora* with prawns, squid, mussels and clams; *risotto al nero di seppie* from the Veneto, coloured and flavoured with the ink of cuttlefish.

Pasta comes in all shapes and sizes, is often home-made and, like risottos, is served with a remarkable range of sauces. *Caoncelli* from Bergamo and Brescia is made with spinach, eggs, cheese, amaretti biscuits and breadcrumbs; *strangolapreti* ('priest stranglers') are elongated dumplings made of spinach, bread, eggs and cheese. In addition to regional sauces you are likely to find the *popular al pomodoro*, tomato sauce flavoured with onion, garlic or basil; *alla carbonara*, with eggs, bacon, Parmesan and pecorino cheeses, and *al ragu*, the Neapolitan meat sauce.

Soups can be a meal in themselves, especially the delicious *zuppa di pesce*, more of a fish stew than a soup. *Minestrone alla milanese* is vegetable soup with rice and bacon; *zuppa pavese* is a clear broth with egg and bread.

Il Secondo

Try and choose seasonal **fish** from local waters, such as *lavarello*, which may come either stuffed with vegetables and herbs, cooked in a sauce such as garlic and almond or capers and tomatoes, simply served on a spit or perhaps puréed and served with bread. Look out also for *luccio mantecato*, cream of pike, accompanied by polenta; *filetto di pesce persico alle erbe aromatiche,* fillet of perch with aromatic herbs; lake trout *(trota)* stuffed with herbs or perhaps baked with olives, capers and anchovies, or simply grilled; and *carpione*, a kind of carp found only in Lake Garda.

Most menus also feature fish from the Italian seas (and beyond), such as *branzino* (bass), *orata* (bream), *sogliola* (sole) *gamberoni* (giant prawns), *calamari* (squid) and *vongole* (clams). Non-lake fish may well be frozen – and some of the more upfront restaurants will indicate this with a star against the item. Smaller fish are served whole at a fixed price, the larger species will be charged by the *etto* (100g) and it's wise to check out the price before ordering.

Salted dried cod is used in dozens of recipes. From the Veneto, for example, comes *baccalà mantecato*, dried salted cod made into a creamy paste with garlic and olive oil and served with polenta – something of an acquired taste. Also from the Veneto and not to everyone's taste is *sarde in saor*,

Practicalities

Normal opening times of restaurants are lunch from 12/12.30–2/3pm, dinner 7.30/8–10pm or even later in main resorts. Expect to pay €1.50–€5 cover charge and in some restaurants a service charge of 10–15 percent.

sardines in a sweet-and-sour sauce.

The main Milanese **meat** specialities are *osso buco*, veal-shank stew; and *costoletta alla milanese*, veal cutlet fried in breadcrumbs (called *wienerschnitzel* in northern Lake Garda). Most menus will feature simply cooked steak, pork, chicken, veal, lamb, duck and often more humble fare such as braised donkey, rabbit casserole, jugged hare or stewed tripe. The choice will vary according to the season. Around Brescia you may come across *lumache alla bresciana*, snails cooked with spinach and served with Parmesan. Polenta often accompanies meat dishes, especially in Trentino and around Bergamo, Brescia and Lake Garda. *Peara* sauce is a Veronese speciality, a blend of breadcrumbs, bone marrow, beef stock, black pepper and Parmesan. The Milanese *cassoeula*, a pork and Savoy cabbage casserole, is served with polenta and traditionally eaten in winter.

Spaghetti alle vongole

Main courses often come with **vegetables** *(contorni)*; salads are ordered and served separately and are almost invariably *verde* (green) or *mista* (mixed). Vegetarian restaurants are a rarity though meat- and fish-free dishes are increasingly available on menus. You might try grilled vegetables as an *antipasto*, then a risotto or pasta with fresh *porcini* or other vegetables.

Desserts don't play a major role on the menus. The usual choice is fruit salad, ice cream, sorbet and perhaps a home-made

Osso bucco with risotto

apple tart or tiramisu (literally 'pick-me-up'), the alcoholic chocolate and coffee gateau from the Veneto.

Cheeses are abundant, from the soft white ricotta from the mountains; the creamy robiolo from the pre-Alpine valleys of Lombardy; the tangy Taleggio from Valsassina (Lake Como); to the hard Parmesan-like grana from the Padua Plain. Panettone, the large cake containing raisins and candied fruit, is a speciality of Milan; *torrone* is a honey and almond nougat originating from Cremona.

WHAT TO DRINK

Lombardy produces some excellent red wines, best of which are the dry, smooth reds from Valtellina on the Swiss/Italian border near Lake Como. The Oltrepò Pavese zone, in the Po Valley south of Pavia, is Italy's third-largest wine producer, noted for good, full-bodied, dry reds; it also produces Pinot sparkling white wine and a large quantity of Riesling. The hilly Franciacorta region bordering Lake Iseo produces good red and white wine, but is best known for its sparkling *spumante*, which makes an excellent aperitif. Lake Garda's best wines are still white and sparkling Bianco di Custoza, and dry red Bardolino, which you can try at the Vinoteca adjoining the Museo del Vino in Bardolino (www.zeni.it) and buy very cheaply in and around the town. The Verona region produces the famous white Soave, red Valpolicella and the lesser-known but top-quality smooth red Recioto, best served with dessert.

A good meal is usually concluded with a *digestivo*, such as a brandy, *grappa* (the variable local firewater made from grape skins) or *limoncello*, made from lemons.

COFFEE BREAK

An Italian café almost invariably serves a decent cup of real coffee. A cappuccino (familiarly called a *cappuccio*), won't be a huge Starbucks-like mug of froth but a normal-sized cup with a generous amount of espresso and a frothy topping. Italians only drink cappuccino for breakfast but are used to foreigners drinking it all day. After around 11am and particularly after meals the locals get their injection of caffeine from a small black espresso.

Tourist hotels often have a DIY machine for 'American coffee' at breakfast time, but normally a waiter will be happy to make you an Italian cappuccino at no extra cost. In a region of people-watching piazzas and mesmerising lake views it's a great temptation to sit for hours over one cup of coffee (or cocktail if you wish), and no one minds if you do. The following is a list of just a few of the different types of coffee served in bars or cafés.

Espresso or *caffè* – small and black
Caffè lungo – weaker coffee
Caffe doppio – double espresso
Caffè latte – milky coffee
Caffè macchiato – small espresso with a dash of milk
Caffè corretto – with grappa, brandy or other liqueur
Caffè freddo – iced coffee
Decaffeinato or *decaff* – decaffeinated coffee

TO HELP YOU ORDER...

A table for one/two/three **Un tavolo per una persona/per due/per tre**
I would like... **Vorrei...**
The bill, please **Il conto, per favore**

aglio garlic
agnello lamb
aragosta lobster
baccalà salted cod
basilica basil
birra beer
bistecca beefsteak
branzino bass
bresaola cured beef
burro butter
capretto kid
cavallo horse
cipolle onions
coniglio rabbit
cozze mussels
fagioli beans
fagiolini green beans
finocchio fennel
formaggio cheese
frittata omelette
frutti di mare seafood
funghi mushrooms
gamberetti shrimps
gamberi prawns
gamberoni giant prawns
gelato ice cream
insalata salad
lumache snails
maiale pork
manzo beef
melanzane aubergine
olio oil
olive olives
orate bream
pane bread
panna cream
patate potatoes
peperoni peppers
pesce fish
piselli peas
pollo chicken
polpo/pólipo octopus
pomodori tomatoes
prosciutto ham
riso rice
salsiccie sausages
sogliola sole
spinaci spinach
trota trout
uova eggs
verdure vegetables
vitello veal
vino wine
zucchini courgettes

PLACES TO EAT

The prices indicated below are a basic guide for a three-course evening meal per person, including wine, cover charge and service.

€€€€	over 65 euros
€€€	45–65 euros
€€	30–45 euros
€	below 30 euros

LAKE MAGGIORE

Borromeo Islands

Belvedere €€€€ *Via di Mezzo, Isola dei Pescatori, tel: 0323 32292,* www.belvedere-isolapescatori.it. An idyllic waterside setting on the charming Isola dei Pescatori, with meals served in the garden, on the verandah or in the lakeview dining room. The restaurant specialises in fresh lake fish such as *laverello* grilled with butter and sage, trout, perch or mixed grill from the lake. By day you get here by ferry, by night the hotel boat will come and collect you from Stresa, Baveno or Pallanza. (Reservations essential for evening meals). If you're tempted to stay, the Belvedere is also a hotel, with attractive, simply furnished lakeview rooms. Open Mar–Nov. Closed Tue in March and Oct.

Cannobio

Grotto Sant'Anna €€ *Via Sant'Anna, 30 (on the road to Valle Cannobina), tel: 0323 70682.* Perched on the edge of the Orrido di Sant'Anna, a spectacular gorge, with a large garden and river-view terrace. The simple excellent value menu offers lake and sea fish, delicious pasta and risotto and desserts to die for. Closed Mon.

Lo Scalo €€€€ *Piazza Vittorio Emanuele III 32, tel: 0323 71480,* www.loscalo.com. Sophisticated restaurant right on the waterfront in a porticoed 14th-century palazzo which once sheltered local fishing boats. Delicious home-made pastas, fish from the lake and a serious wine list. Closed Mon, except evenings mid-summer, and Tue lunch.

Mergozzo

Piccolo Lago €€€€ *Via Filippo Turati 87, Fondotoce, Lake Mergozzo, tel: 0323 586792,* www.piccololago.it. The 'Little Lake' restaurant boasts two Michelin stars and a beautiful setting on the tiny Lago di Mergozzo, between Mergozzo and Fondotoce. Traditional Piedmontese dishes, rich risottos and trout, pike and perch from the lake are elegantly prepared and presented. This is also a hotel with 12 modern rooms and lakeside pool. Closed Mon–Tue and lunch on Wed.

Pallanza

Osteria del Riccio €€€ *Vicolo dell'Arco 1, tel: 0323 558842.* A cosy restaurant enjoying lovely lake views. Seafood is the speciality here but the rest of the menu is also definitely worth a try. Open for dinner Tue–Fri and for dinner and lunch Sat–Sun.

Ristorante Milano €€€€ *Corso Zannitello 2/4, tel: 0323 556816,* www.ristorantemilanolagomaggiore.it. Frighteningly pricey but worth splashing out for the great lakeside location by the old harbour, the exquisite fish dishes and the succulent meat from Piedmont. Everything here is freshly sourced, the setting is elegant and the service faultless. Closed Mon dinner and Tue.

Stresa

Il Vicoletto €€ *Vicolo del Poncivo 3, tel: 0323 932102;* www.ristorantevicoletto.com. Tucked away in an alley *(vicoletto)* off the main square, this tiny restaurant with its contemporary menu bucks the trend of Stresa's pizzeria and spaghetti-oriented restaurants. Emphasis here is very much on quality rather than quantity – the menu is small, and the helpings are not huge (you'll have room for the heavenly desserts). Expect simple pastas, and roast meat and fish, all using top quality ingredients. Space is limited inside and out, so reservations are recommended. Closed Thu and mid-Jan–Feb.

La Botte € *Via Mazzini 6/8, tel: 0323 30462.* 'The Barrel' is a simple little wood-panelled eatery serving good-value Piedmontese dishes, hearty steaks, pasta and pizzas. Inside tables only, very popular and often crowded. Closed Wed.

Osteria degli Amici €€ *Via A.M. Bolongaro 31, tel: 0323 30453.* Popular for pizzas cooked in a wood-fired oven, pastas and risottos, steak or grilled fish. For ambience opt for a table outside under the vines – there are outdoor heaters for cooler evenings. Closed Wed.

LAKE COMO

Bellagio

Barchetta €€€ *Salita Mella 18 13, tel: 031 951389,* www.ristorantebarchetta.com. A long-established and consistently good trattoria up a stepped alley from the waterfront. The menu features creative pastas, creamy risottos and delicious fresh fish. A heated terrace means you can enjoy the views even on cool days. For simpler fare, snacks and pizzas there is a separate area open at lunchtime.

Silvio €€ *Via Paolo Carcano 10–12, tel: 031 950322,* www.bellagiosilvio.com. Above the gardens of Villa Melzi, on the main Bellagio to Como road, this is worth the detour for the freshest of fish, caught by Silvio's family, and the peaceful setting above the lake. *Taglioni al lavarello* (pasta with lake fish) and *semifreddo di grappa e uvetta* (ice cream with grappa and raisins) are house specialities. This is also a hotel with modestly priced rooms. Closed winter.

Brunate

Trattoria del Cacciatore € *Via Manzoni 22, tel: 031 220012,* www.trattoriadelcacciatore.it. Leave the bustle of Como and take the 7-minute cable car ride up to the hilltop village of Brunate. This is a delightful rustic, inconspicuous trattoria (follow signs or ask the way), with red tablecloths and a wisteria-clad pergola. Meals are simple affairs, with meat antipasti, pasta and meat casseroles with mushrooms and polenta. Closed Tue and Sun dinner. In winter only open by reservation.

Como

Er Più €€€ *35/56 Via Castellini 21, tel: 031 272154;* www.erpiucomo.it. One of the few good restaurants in Como, this is a haven for fish fans. You can have it smoked, salted, fried, oven-cooked, marinated, in a soup or in a stew. The fish comes from both lake and sea, and the menu typically features everything from lobster, scallops and clams to seabass and salmon. Desserts, created by the patisserie chef since 1974, are irresistible. To save on cost go at lunch time when the set menu is half the price of the evening meals. Closed Tue, occasionally in Aug, and one week in Jan.

La Colombetta €€€€ *Via Diaz 40, tel: 031 262703;* www.colombetta.it. A family-run restaurant housed in the very romantic setting of a former church in Como's historic centre. Excellent contemporary dishes and an extensive wine list. George Clooney is a regular there. Closed Sunday.

Isola Comancina

Locanda dell'Isola Comacina €€€€ *Isola Comacina, tel: 0344 55083,* www.comacina.it. You are ferried to the deserted island from Sala Comacina and served a rustic lunch of antipasti, grilled trout and salmon, chicken cooked in a wood oven and dessert. The meal ends with a rite-of-fire to exorcise the curse put on the island in the 12th century by the Bishop of Como. A rather gimmicky experience, but unique nonetheless. Closed winter and Tue off-season.

Varenna

Il Cavatappi €€ *Via XX Settembre, tel: 0341 815349,* www.cavatappivarenna.it. 'The Corkscrew' is a minute eatery on a little alleyway with just five tables. Simple but delicious cuisine, a well-stocked wine cellar and a very cosy atmosphere. Mon–Tue dinner only, closed Wed Sept–Apr.

Vecchia Varenna €€€ *Contrada Scoscesa 10, tel: 0341 830793,* www.vecchiavarenna.it. Irresistible waterside setting with lake and mountain views and an excellent choice of fish. You can have it stuffed with vegetables and herbs, on a spit, in fishcakes, baked with olives and capers or flavouring risottos. Carnivores are not ignored – there is braised donkey, stewed rabbit or – for more conventional tastes – steak and pork. Daily lunch and dinner, closed Jan.

LAKE GARDA

Desenzano del Garda

Caffè Italia €€€ *Piazza Malvezzi 19, tel: 030 9141243,* www.ristorantecaffeitalia.it. Historic café in the centre where you can grab a quick morning cappuccino and brioche at the bar with the locals, enjoy a light lunch on the terrace or a blow-out seven-course *menu degustazione* (tasting menu). The piles of prawns, oysters, scallops and other seafood sitting on ice are more than likely to tempt you.

Esplanade €€€€ *Via Lario 3, tel: 030 9143361;* www.ristorante-esplanade.com. One of Lake Garda's top restaurants where Chef Massimo Fezzardi's cuisine combines tradition with creativity. Enjoy a stunning lake setting and a menu typically featuring *millefeuille* of artichokes with roast scampi and purée of anchovy, salt-crusted Piedmont fillet of beef and duck ravioli with rosemary and goose liver. Closed Wed.

Gargnano

La Tortuga di Orietta €€€€ *Via XXIV Maggio 5, tel: 0365 71251,* www.ristorantelatortuga.it. Save this one for a special occasion and since it's very small make sure to book a table. In the charming fishing village of Gargnano this rustic restaurant serves exquisite dishes and great wines. Fish predominates but you can also find meat antipasti and main courses such as carpaccio of duck and lamb with rosemary and thyme or fillet of veal with truffles. Closed Tue.

Moniga del Garda

Agriturismo del Trenta €€ *Via Mazzane 2, Moniga del Garda (north of Desenzano del Garda), tel: 0365 503395,* www.agriturismo30.com. Enjoy great value set meals and lake views from the vine-clad terrace of this rural *agriturismo*. Many of the ingredients, including fruit, veg and wheat flour are produced on the farm. Delightful staff complete the picture. Booking is essential.

Riva del Garda

Ristorante Restel de Fer €€€ *Via Restel de Fer 10, tel: 0464 553481,* www.resteldefer.com. Delightful rustic trattoria and inn, run by the Meneghelli family since 1400. Many of the dishes are based on ancient Trentino recipes. Fish comes from Lake Garda and the Trentino rivers, meat is organic, vegetables are home-grown and the extra virgin oil is produced from the family olive grove. Try the Trentino wines from the well-stocked cellar and round off the meal with a grappa. Daily for dinner, lunch for small groups with a reservation. Closed Nov.

Sirmione

Risorgimento €€€ *Piazza Carducci 5–6, tel: 030 916325,* www.risorgimento-sirmione.com. Sirmione is packed with takeaway pizza places but for proper food and smart service the Risorgimento is the place to go. On a lively piazza near where the ferries come and go, it has a wide choice of fish, served with pasta and risotto, or simply grilled, as well as flambéed steaks and mouth-watering desserts. Closed Tue.

Torri del Benaco

Gardesana €€€ *Piazza Calderini 20, tel: 045 7225411,* http://gardesana.eu. This historic hotel's (see page 140) lakeside setting is as delightful as ever, overlooking the harbour and castle. The menu offers up fresh fish from the lake, along with sea fish, giant prawns, meat dishes and pizza. Open mid-Mar–mid-Oct. Closed Mon.

Lake Orta – Orta San Giulio

Al Boeuc € *Via Bersani 28, tel: 0332 915854.* Ancient, atmospheric tavern where you can sample good wines, *prosciutto*, *bruschetta* or *bagna cauda*, a warm garlic and anchovy dip served with cruditées. There are some tables outside lining the pleasant cobbled alley. Closed Thu.

Taverna Antico Agnello €€ *Via Solari 5, Miasino, tel: 0322 980527,* www.ristoranteanticoagnello.com. Charming rustic trattoria with emphasis on meat dishes (horse and donkey among them) and specialities from Piedmont. Closed Wed.

Villa Crespi €€€€ *Via G. Fava 18, Orta San Giulio, tel: 0322 911902,* www.villacrespi.it. An exclusive Moorish villa hotel (see page 141) with a Neapolitan chef who sources the finest ingredients: mozzarella from southern Italy, shrimps from San Remo, truffles from Alba, locally grown fresh fruit and vegetables. His creative dishes – many of which are Mediterranean – have earned the restaurant two Michelin stars. Feast on Sicilian scampi in Martini sauce, ravioli with clams and caviar, veal fillet with black truffle – washed down with wine from the 83-page wine list. For the ultimate gourmet sensation opt for the 10-course tasting menu. Closed Mon.

CITIES

Bergamo

Colleoni & dell'Angelo €€€€ *Piazza Vecchia 7, Città Alta, tel: 035 232596,* www.colleonidellangelo.com. Elegant palace setting with a much sought-after terrace on the stunning central square of the upper city. Exquisite pasta dishes on offer include Bergamo's *casoncelli*, ravioli with sage, butter and almonds parmesan, linguine with sea urchins, Beluga caviar, ravioli stuffed with pigeon breast and foie gras with pistaccio. These can be followed by sea bass or gilthead in a sea-salt crust or rack of lamb in a black truffle crust. Closed Mon and two weeks in August.

Da Mimmo €€€ *Via B. Colleoni 17, Città Alta, tel: 035 218535,* www.ristorantemimmo.com. In the same family for half a century, Da Mimmo sources the finest raw materials from Bergamo's market and serves strictly traditional regional fare: home-made Bergamasche pastas, outstanding fish dishes, rabbit and polenta, ageing *bagoss* cheese, bread cooked in wood ovens, delicious pizzas and home-made desserts. You can dine within the 14th-century *palazzo* or in the garden on summer evenings. It's a favourite haunt of locals so reservations (which can be done online) are advisable. Closed Tue lunch.

Elav Kitchen and Beer €€ *Via Solata 8, tel: 035 017 2871.* Run by an independent brewery, this restaurant-bar with modern furnishings is hidden on a back street of Bergamo's Citta Altà. Set menus present four courses, each with a beer pairing. The food is fresh and local, with risotto and pancetta pasta making regular appearances. Tue–Sun, dinner only.

Trattoria 3 Torri €€ *Piazza Mercato del Fieno 7, tel: 035 244474.* A cosy, characterful eatery with bare-brick walls and arched roof, serving a good polenta del Bergamì, among other local pasta dishes. The menu is small but has a good range of meat and vegetarian options. Closed Wed.

Vineria Cozzi €€ *Via B. Colleoni 22a, tel: 035 238836,* www.vineriacozzi.it. Inviting *bottega* popular for its huge choice of Italian wines and varied menu offering *antipasti*, vegetarian dishes such as polenta and *porcini* mushrooms, a selection of cold meats or cheeses and some delicious pastas. The *menu degustazione*, comprising four courses, has an excellent choice of house specialities with wines to go with them.

Brescia and Province

Caffè Floriam €€ *Via Gasparo da Salò 3, Brescia, tel: 030 41314,* www.caffefloriamrestaurant.it. In the heart of the historic centre near Piazza della Loggia, this is a long-established, welcoming café-restaurant serving traditional home-cooked dishes, including 11 different risottos.

Varese

Ristorante Bologna €€ *Albergo Bologna, Via Broggi 7, tel: 0332 234362,* www.albergobologna.it. A central, family-run hotel restaurant offering good-value set menus, featuring fresh pasta such as *tagliolini alla crema di asparagi* (with cream of asparagus), *gnocchi con salsa gialla di noce e zafferano* (with yellow walnut and saffron sauce), followed by meat or fish, and one of the creamy, calorific home-made desserts. Wine, coffee and a *digestivo* are thrown in too. Closed Sat and third Sun of the month.

Vecchia Riva €€€ *Via G. Macchi 146, Schiranna, Lago di Varese, tel: 0332 329300,* www.vecchiariva.com. Set on the banks of the unspoilt Lake Varese, Vecchia Riva has a sheltered garden and serves a large spread of regional *antipasti*, good fish, risotto and pasta dishes. The restaurant is attached to a small three-star hotel that offers functional modern rooms.

Verona

12 Apostoli €€€€ *Vicolo Corticella San Marco 3, tel: 045 596999,* www.12apostoli.it. Charming, traditional restaurant in an 18th century palazzo, with frescoed vaulted ceilings and classic cuisine. It is named after 12 friends who used to do business here in the mid-18th century over a simple dish of pasta or beans and a glass of wine. Closed Mon, Sun dinner and 20 days in Aug.

Al Bersagliere €€ *Via Dietro Pallone 1, tel: 045 8004824,* www.trattoriaalbersagliere.it. Tuck into top-notch Veronese and Venetian fare: polenta with home-cured salami, pasta and *fagioli* beans, *bigoli* (spaghetti-like pasta) with duck ragù or simply-grilled steak and fish. The speciality of stewed horse meat with polenta follows a Veronese recipe of the 15th century. There are three rooms, a summer garden and a 12th century cellar with 200 labels. Closed Mon and Sun.

Casa Perbellini €€€€ *Piazza San Zeno 16, tel: 045 8780860,* www.casaperbellini.com. The concept restaurant of multiple-starred chef Giancarlo Perbellini in the heart of Verona's historic centre. Pricey but excellent Italian cuisine. Closed Sun and Mon, 10 days in Feb and 20 days in Aug.

A–Z TRAVEL TIPS

A SUMMARY OF PRACTICAL INFORMATION

A Accommodation 115
Airports 116
B Bicycle hire 117
Budgeting for your trip 117
C Camping 117
Car hire 118
Climate 118
Clothing 119
Crime and safety 119
D Disabled travellers 119
Driving 120
E Electricity 121
Embassies and consulates 121
Emergencies 121
G Getting there 122
Guides and tours 122
H Health and medical care 122
L Language 123
LGBTQ travellers 125
M Maps 125
Media 125
Money 126
O Opening hours 126
P Police 127
Post offices 127
Public holidays 127
R Religion 128
S Smoking 128
T Telephones 128
Time zones 129
Tipping 130
Toilets 130
Tourist information 130
Transport 131
V Visa and entry requirements 132
W Websites and internet access 133
Y Youth hostels 133

A

ACCOMMODATION

Accommodation in the region is plentiful, with grandiose lakeside villa hotels, romantic retreats in the hills, farmhouses, simple bed and breakfasts, and self-catering villas and apartments. Prices vary according to the season, being at their highest in midsummer. Many of the hotels on the lakes close in winter.

The busiest times are Easter, July and August, but for some hotels high season is now from Easter all the way through to the end of September. It is advisable to book well ahead throughout the season, especially for lakeside hotels. During the summer some smaller establishments may require you to stay for a minimum of three nights, and those with restaurants may only offer half- or full-board rates. A deposit of at least one night's stay, payable by credit card, is usually requested. Failure to turn up or to inform the hotel in advance of cancellation will normally incur the loss of a night's deposit.

If you arrive on spec, local tourist offices will advise on available accommodation and may do the booking for you. If possible, check out the guest room before committing to a reservation. Rooms can vary hugely, both in size and outlook. Prices normally reflect the difference, and it's usually worth stretching the budget to secure the more desirable rooms. In lakeside resorts, hotels are often located across the main road from the lake, with noisy rooms at the front. Breakfast is generally included in the overnight room rate. Depending on the category of hotel this will vary from a dull crusty roll with packaged butter and jam to a great spread of cereals, cheeses, cold cuts, yoghurts, croissants, home-made pastries and fresh fruit. If breakfast is not included in the room rate it is usually better value to pop out for a cappuccino and croissant in the local café.

An appealing alternative to hotel accommodation is *agriturismi*, working farms and other rural properties which rent out rooms or self-contained apartments to tourists. These are an excellent choice for exploring peaceful rural regions and for active holidays such as walking, cycling, horse-riding, wine-tasting or milking the cows. Some agriturismi offer breakfast and an evening meal, which is based on home-grown produce. Meals are communal affairs, often around the kitchen table. However, not all *agriturismi* conform to the picturesque farmhouse image – many are modern properties in unremarkable settings. Details of *agriturismi* are supplied by local tourist offices – or visit www.agriturist.com or www.agriturismo.net.

In recent years the region has seen a huge increase in the number of Bed and Breakfasts in private homes. These usually offer better value than hotels as well as the opportunity to get to know the owners and speak some Italian. For information, visit www.bbitalia.it.

AIRPORTS

The lakes region has no less than five airports, including the three that serve Milan. For the lakes in the west of the region (Orta, Maggiore and Como), the most convenient arrival points are Milan's Malpensa airport, 50km (31 miles) northwest of Milan (www.airportmalpensa.com) or Orio al Serio airport at Bergamo, 48km (30 miles) northeast of Milan (www.sacbo.it). This is also the ideal arrival point if you are heading to Lake Iseo. For Milan, Linate airport (www.milanolinate.eu), 10km (6 miles) to the east, is by far the closest airport to the city.

For Lake Garda's western shore, the quickest gateway is Brescia's airport (www.aeroportobrescia.it), 20km (12.5 miles) southeast of Brescia, which confusingly has three different names: 'Gabriele d'Annunzio', 'Brescia-Montichiari' and 'Verona (Brescia)'. If you are hiring a car the airport is also worth considering for access to Verona (52km/32 miles), Cremona (47km/29 miles) and Bergamo (65km/40 miles). Another useful gateway for Lake Garda, particularly the eastern shore, is Valerio Catullo Airport, also called Verona-Villafranca (www.aeroportoverona.it), which is only 15km (9.5 miles) from Verona. For the east shores of Lake Garda you could also consider the Venice airports of Marco Polo and Treviso which are less than an hour away.

Bergamo's Orio al Serio airport, used by Ryanair and other low-cost airlines, is linked by a half-hourly shuttle bus service to both Bergamo, 5km (3 miles) away, and to Milan's Stazione Centrale (Central Station). Gabriele d'Annunzio airport is linked to Brescia by regular shuttle buses, but to Verona by a very limited service. From Verona's Valerio Catullo airport there are buses to the city's railway station every 20 minutes from 6.30am to 11.30pm.

B

BICYCLE HIRE

Bikes can be hired in all the towns and resorts, but prices are quite steep. Local tourist offices can supply details of local bike-hire outlets as well as trail guides in popular biking regions. Hills and mountains have signposted tracks of varying degrees of difficulty. A few hotels lend their guests bikes free of charge.

BUDGETING FOR YOUR TRIP

In high season you can expect to pay around €150–250 for a comfortable double room with bath, €90–150 in a simple hotel. A good three-course meal with wine in a restaurant will cost from €30–60, a light lunch €10–25. In general the best-value accommodation and restaurants are located away from the lakefronts. Coffee and soft drinks are €1.50–4, beer € 3–5, while an aperitif or cocktail with canapés is €3–10. It is worth bearing in mind that, as in the rest of Italy, coffee or drinks taken at the bar are far cheaper than those taken at a table with waiter service. Entrance charges to museums, archaeological sites and gardens vary from €2–12; entrance is free for EU citizens under 18 and over 65. Opera tickets in Verona cost from €20–200.

C

CAMPING

Campsites are dotted around all the main lakes and range from basic sites to four-star affairs with swimming pools, restaurants, bungalows as well as tents and organised activities. Lake Garda has by far the widest choice, with sites all round the shores and a profusion in the south. Details are available at www.camping.it where you can book online. Campsites are normally open from April to September and are at their most crowded from mid-July to late August.

CAR HIRE

Hiring a car is essential if you're planning a touring holiday, though the traffic and tunnels along many of the lakeside roads don't lead to leisurely driving. You must be over 21 and you will need a full, valid driver's license, held for at least a year. Car-hire bookings made in advance on the internet work out cheaper than hiring on arrival. In high season a small economy car will cost from around €250 a week, including third-party liability and taxes, but excluding insurance excess. Make sure you check all extras when comparing quotes from different companies. The major car-hire companies have offices in the main cities and airports. There is a small additional charge for an extra driver. Credit-card imprints are taken as a deposit and are normally the only form of payment acceptable. 'Inclusive' prices do not normally include personal accident insurance or insurance against damage to windscreens, tyres and wheels.

CLIMATE

The holiday season for the lakes is Easter to October. The best time to go is spring, early summer or autumn, ideal times being May, June and September when it's warm and sunny but not as crowded, hot or muggy as midsummer. In July and August temperatures can soar to 30°C, though the lakes, with a gentle breeze, are slightly cooler than the cities. The wettest months are October and November. Winters are foggy and cold with chilly winds from the Alps. Most places around the lakes close down for the season and ferry services are limited.

	J	F	M	A	M	J	J	A	S	O	N	D
°C	5	8	13	18	23	27	29	29	24	17	10	6
°F	40	46	56	65	74	80	84	85	75	63	51	43

CLOTHING

Bring light to medium-weight clothing and rainwear during spring and autumn, and pack a jacket for summer evenings. Remember that Italy's churches are places of worship as well as repositories of art and architecture, and you should dress respectably – shorts, miniskirts, bare shoulders and midriffs are frowned upon and may even mean that you are not allowed entry.

CRIME AND SAFETY

It is wise to take simple precautions against pickpockets, especially in the larger cities. Avoid carrying large amounts of cash around with you and leave important documents and valuables in the hotel safe. Keep a firm hold of handbags, especially when using public transport or shopping at markets. For insurance purposes, theft and loss must be reported straightaway to the police. In case of theft take photocopies of flight tickets, driving licence, passport and insurance documents.

D

DISABLED TRAVELLERS

Italy is not easy for disabled visitors, but is making slow progress in improving transport, accommodation and buildings.

New trains and buses are low-level, and more museums now have lifts, ramps and adapted toilets, and recent laws require restaurants, bars and hotels to provide spacious and specially adapted toilets. The new legislation does not, however, necessarily cover access to the facilities.

Access at Last is a 'one-stop-shop' for accessible accommodation and services with a worldwide database of places to stay: www.accessatlast.com.

DRIVING

If taking your own car from the UK, you should allow for tolls on French, Swiss, German and Italian motorways. To take your car into Italy, you will need an international driving licence or valid national one, car registration and insurance documents, a red warning triangle and reflective vest in case of breakdown, a national identity sticker for your car, and headlamp deflectors. Tolls are levied on the motorway but it's worth the relatively small expense to cover ground fast. Signposting on main and rural roads is quite good, but beware of reckless drivers and motorcyclists.

Rules of the road. Drive on the right, pass on the left. Speed limits in Italy are 50kmh (30mph) in towns and built-up areas, 90kmh (55mph) on main roads and 130kmh (80mph) on motorways. At roundabouts the traffic from the right has the right of way. Seat belts are compulsory in the front and back, and children should be properly restrained. The use of hand-held mobile telephones while driving is prohibited. The blood alcohol limit is 0.08 percent and police occasionally take random breath tests.

Breakdowns. In case of general emergencies call 113, or for breakdown assistance call the Automobile Club of Italy on 116. The club has an efficient 24-hour service which is available to foreigners.

Petrol. Petrol is readily available, though many service stations close for three hours over the lunch period. On main roads there are plenty of 24-hour stations with self-service dispensers accepting euro notes and major credit cards but instructions are normally in Italian only. The majority of service stations accept credit cards.

Parking. Parking is not expensive but it can be difficult finding spaces in the centre of towns and lakeside resorts at busy times of the year. Parking in towns is controlled by meters or scratch cards, available from tobacconists and bars. The larger towns have multi-storey car parks. Some free parking is controlled by parking discs (if you have hired a car a disc will be provided). Parking in Milan is notoriously difficult and to be discouraged.

E

ELECTRICITY

220V/50Hz AC is standard. Sockets take two-pin, round-pronged plugs. UK appliances will require an adaptor, American 11V appliances a transformer.

EMBASSIES AND CONSULATES

If you lose your passport or need other help, contact your nearest national embassy or consulate.

Australia: Australian Consulate, Via Borgogna 2, 3rd floor, 20122 Milan, tel: 02 7767 4200, www.italy.embassy.gov.au

Canada: Canadian Consulate, Piazza Cavour 3, 6th floor, 20121 Milan, tel: 02 6269 4238, www.international.gc.ca

Ireland: Irish Honorary Consulate, Piazza S. Pietro in Gessate 2, 20122 Milan, tel: 02 5518 7569, www.dfa.ie/irish-embassy/italy

New Zealand: New Zealand Consulate, Via Terraggio 17, 20123 Milan, tel: 02 7217 0001, www.nzembassy.com/italy

South Africa: South African Consulate, Vicolo San Giovanni, Sul Moro 4, 20121 Milan, tel: 02 885 8581, www.sudafrica.it

UK: British Consulate, Via San Paolo 7, 20121 Milan, tel: 02 723 001, http://ukinitaly.fco.gov.uk

US: US Consulate, Via Principe Amedeo 2/10, 20121 Milan, tel: 02 290 351, https://it.usembassy.gov

EMERGENCIES

Police 112
General Emergency 113
Fire 115
Ambulance 118

G

GETTING THERE

By air. Ryanair, www.ryanair.com, currently flies from four UK airports to 'Milan-Bergamo' (Bergamo's Orio al Serio airport); and also from Stansted and Birmingham to Verona (Brescia). EasyJet, www.easyjet.com, flies from Gatwick to Milan's Linate and Malpensa, from Luton to Malpensa and from Gatwick to Verona. British Airways, www.ba.com and the Italian national airline Alitalia, www.alitalia.com, have regular flights from Heathrow to both Linate and Malpensa; BA also flies from Manchester to Malpensa, and from Gatwick to Valerio Catullo (Verona).

By car. The quickest route to Milan from the UK channel ports takes a minimum of 12 hours, over a distance of 1,040km (650 miles). For route planning and details on the cost of petrol, road tolls (levied on French and Italian motorways) and the Swiss motorway road tax, visit www.viamichelin.com.

By rail. You can get to Milan in 12 hours from London St Pancras via Paris on Eurostar (full details on www.seat61.com). From Milan there are fast train services to all the main lakes. For information on tickets, rail passes and to book online, contact the Italian train operator Trenitalia (www.trenitalia.com).

GUIDES AND TOURS

Local tourist offices, travel agencies and hotels can provide details of guides and tours. There is no shortage of choice whether it's a guided city tour, a ferry cruise, a Romeo and Juliet tour in Verona or an excursion to the cellars and vineyards in the wine-producing regions.

H

HEALTH AND MEDICAL CARE

All EU countries have reciprocal arrangements for reclaiming the costs of medical services, and residents should obtain the European Health Insurance Card (available in the UK from post offices or online at www.ehic.org.

uk). This only covers you for medical care, not for emergency repatriation costs or additional expenses such as accommodation and flights for anyone travelling with you. To cover all eventualities a travel insurance policy is advisable, and for non-EU residents, essential. For insurance claims keep all receipts for medical treatment and any medicines prescribed. Vaccinations are not needed for Italy, but take with you sunscreen and mosquito repellent in the summer. Tap water is safe to drink unless you see the sign *acqua non potabile*. A pharmacy (*farmacia*) is identified by a green cross. All main towns offer a 24-hour pharmacy service, with a night-time and Sunday rota. After-hour locations are listed in local papers and posted on all pharmacy doors. Italian pharmacists are well-trained to deal with minor ailments and although they do not stock quantities of foreign medicines they can usually supply the local equivalent. If you need a doctor (*medico*) ask at the pharmacy or at your hotel. For serious cases or emergencies, dial 118 for an ambulance or head for the *Pronto Soccorso* (Accident and Emergency) of the local hospital. This will also deal with emergency dental treatment.

L

LANGUAGE

Staff in hotels and shops in the main resorts speak English, but a smattering of Italian will come in useful if you're off-the-beaten-track. On the Swiss side of the lakes less English is spoken than German.

What time does the train/bus leave for the city centre? **A che ora parte il treno/pullman per in centro?**

Is there a campsite near here? **C'è un campeggio qui vicino?**

I would like to hire a car **Vorrei noleggiare una macchina**

for one day **per un giorno**

for one week **per una settimana**

I want full insurance. **Voglio l'assicurazione completa.**
I want to report a theft. **Vorrei denunciare un furto.**
My wallet/passport/ticket has been stolen **Mi hanno rubato il portafoglio/il passaporto/il biglietto**
I've had a breakdown **Ho avuto un guasto**
There's been an accident **C'è stato un incidente**
Fill it up please **Faccia il pieno per favore**
Super/normal **super/normale**
Lead-free/diesel **senza piombo/ gasolio**
Where's the nearest car park? **Dov'è il parcheggio più vicino?**
Can I park here? **Posso parcheggiare qui?**
Are we on the right road for...? **Siamo sulla strada giusta per...?**
I need a doctor/dentist **Ho bisogno di un medico/dentista**
Where is the nearest chemist? **Dov'è la farmacia più vicina?**
I want to change some pounds/dollars **Desidero cambiare delle sterline/dei dollari**
Do you accept traveller's cheques? **Accetta traveller's cheques?**
Can I pay with a credit card? **Posso pagare con la carta di credito?**
Where is the bank? **Dov'è la banca?**
Where's the nearest police station? **Dov'è il posto di polizia più vicino?**
Where's the nearest post office? **Dov'è l'ufficio postale più vicino?**
I'd like a stamp. **Desidero un francobollo.**
When's the next bus/train to ...? **Quando parte il prossimo autobus/treno per....?**
Where can I buy a ticket? **Dov'è posso comprare un biglietto?**
single (one-way) **andata**

return **andata e ritorno**
Thank you, this is for you. **Grazie, questo è per lei.**
Keep the change. **Tenga il resto.**
Where are the toilets? **Dove sono i gabinetti?**
Where is the tourist office? **Dov'è l'ufficio turistico?**

LGBTQ TRAVELLERS

Milan, along with Bologna, is the most gay-friendly city in Italy. The lakes region, however, is more conservative and, although not necessarily averse to gay couples travelling together, the locals do not always tolerate overt displays of affection. Larger towns like Brescia have gay bars and clubs. ArciGay, Via Bezzecca 3, Milan, tel: 02 54122225, www.arcigay.it, the Italian gay organisation, has centres in Verona, Brescia, Cremona and Mantua as well as Milan. For an excellent guide to gay life and tourism in Italy, visit the website www.gayfriendlyitaly.com.

M

MAPS

Touring Club Italiano (TCI) produces the detailed, easy-to-read 1:200,000 map of Lombardy which covers all the main lakes apart from Garda. Local tourist offices can normally provide you with free town and area maps.

MEDIA

Newspapers. English-language newspapers can be found in main towns and resorts, usually on the day of publication. National newspapers include the Milan-based centre-right daily *Corriere della Sera* (www.corriere.it) and its centre-left rival, *La Repubblica* (www.repubblica.it).

Television and radio. Most hotels provide satellite TV, which broadcasts 24-hour English-language news channels. The Italian state TV network, RAI (Radio Televisione Italiana), broadcasts three TV channels, RAI 1, 2 and 3, which compete with many private channels pouring out soaps, films, quiz shows and nonstop ads. The state-run radio stations, RAI 1, 2 and 3, mainly broadcast news, chat and music.

MONEY

Currency. The unit of currency in Italy is the euro (€) divided into 100 cents. Euro notes come in denominations of 500, 200, 100, 50, 20, 10 and 5; coins come in denominations of 2 and 1 euros, then 50, 20, 10, 5, 2 and 1 cents. In Switzerland the currency is the Swiss franc. In Swiss resorts you can usually pay with euros but your change will be in Swiss francs, and normally at a poor exchange rate.

Exchange facilities. Banks and post offices tend to offer the best rates, followed by exchange offices and hotels.

Credit cards and ATMs. The major international credit cards are accepted in the majority of hotels and restaurants, stores and supermarkets, but some smaller places only accept cash. ATMs (Bancomats) are widespread, but banks take a hefty commission – it is usually better value to use cash only when essential and pay off larger amounts such as restaurant bills and pricier items in shops by credit card.

Traveller's cheques and Cash Passports. Traveller's cheques are not as widely accepted as they used to be in Italy and are less convenient than Cash Passports (prepaid travel money cards). These offer the same security as traveller's cheques and if lost or stolen can be quickly replaced and the full amount refunded. The card can be used to withdraw cash at ATMs or pay hotels, restaurants and shops.

O

OPENING HOURS

Banks generally open Mon–Fri 8am–1.30pm and 3–4pm (afternoon opening times may vary). Banks at airports and main stations usually have longer opening hours and are open at weekends.

Museums have varying opening hours; the main ones open all day every

day, but some small museums close for 2–3 hours over the lunch period and all day on Monday.
Villas/Gardens usually open all day every day in season.
Churches normally close at lunch time (noon–3pm or later). Sightseeing on Sunday morning, when services take place, is discouraged.
Shops are normally open Mon–Sat 9am–1pm and 3.30/4pm– 7.30/8pm. In main cities many shops open all day, and on Sundays too.

P

POLICE

The city police or *polizia urbana* regulate traffic and enforce laws, while the *carabinieri* are the armed military police who handle law and order. The *polizia stradale* patrol the highways and other roads. In an emergency the *carabinieri* can be reached on 112 – or you can ring the general emergency number, 113.

POST OFFICES

Post offices normally open Mon–Fri 8.15am–2pm, Sat 8.15am– noon or 2pm. Stamps *(francobolli)* can also be bought from tobacconists.

PUBLIC HOLIDAYS

Shops, banks, museums and galleries usually close on the days listed below. When a national holiday falls on a Friday or a Monday, Italians may make a *ponte* (bridge) or long weekend.
January 1 *Capodanno* New Year's Day
January 6 *Epifania* Epiphany
March/April *Pasqua* Easter
March/April *Lunedì di Pasqua* Easter Monday
25 April *Festa della Liberazione* Liberation Day
1 May *Festa del Lavoro* Labour Day
2 June *Festa della Repubblica* Republic Day
15 August *Ferragosto* Assumption Day

1 November *Ognissanti* All Saints' Day
8 December *L'Immacolata Concezione* Feast of the Immaculate Conception
25 December *Natale* Christmas Day
26 December *Santo Stefano* St Stephen's Day

R

RELIGION

Like the rest of Italy the region is primarily Roman Catholic. The church still plays a major role in the community though numbers of regular worshippers have been in decline for some years. Local patron saints' days are celebrated, such as San Giovanni Battista on Lake Como, but religious festivals are not as commonplace as in southern Italy. Milan has congregations of all the main religions (for details consult www.hellomilano.it under the 'Worship' section in Useful Information).

S

SMOKING

Smoking in Italy is prohibited in all public places including restaurants, bars and cafés.

T

TELEPHONES

Telecom Italia public telephones are widespread and have instructions in English. Calls are made with a pre-paid phone card (*scheda* or *carta telefónica*) available in denominations of €5, €10 and €20 from Telecom offices, tobacconists, newsstands and vending machines. Many phones also accept payment by credit card.

Pre-paid international telephone cards (from €5), available at post offices, travel agents and other outlets are far better value if you are phoning abroad. With these you call a free phone number, dial the PIN code on your card and then the number (clear instructions are given in English). Calls can also be made with a charge card bought from your telephone company prior to travel. This is useful for telephoning from hotels which levy hefty surcharges on long-distance calls.

When phoning abroad, dial the international code, followed by the city or area code and then the number. Off-peak rate for international calls in Italy is Mon–Sat 10pm–8am, Sun 1pm–Mon 8am. For an English-speaking operator and international reverse charge calls, dial 170 and for international directory enquiries dial 176. Numbers beginning 800 are free. To call Italy from abroad dial the country code, followed by the area code and then the number. Italian area codes have all been incorporated into the numbers, so even if you are calling from the same town that you are telephoning, the code must be included.

Mobile phones (cellphones). In order to function within Italy some mobiles need to be activated with a roaming facility or need to be 'unblocked' for use abroad. Check with your mobile company before leaving. Charges for using a UK- or EU-based mobile to make and receive calls and texts, and browse the internet elsewhere in the EU were scrapped in 2017. It was unclear at the time of writing whether UK-based companies will continue to uphold this after the UK leaves the European Union. For phones from outside the EU charges may still be high for all services. You can set your mobile to the cheapest network on arrival. You can also bar incoming calls, or on some mobiles limit them to specified numbers. If you are in Italy for some time it's worth purchasing an Italian SIM 'pay as you go' *(scheda pre-pagata)* with a new mobile number for the length of your stay. To do so you will need your passport or ID card. The SIM card can be bought from any mobile shop in Italy. UK customers can purchase a card before you go via www.uk2abroad.com and keep your mobile number.

Country codes. Australia +61; Ireland +353; New Zealand +64; South Africa +27, UK +44; US and Canada +1.

TIME ZONES

Italy is one hour ahead of Greenwich Mean Time (GMT). From the last

Sunday in March to the last Sunday in October, clocks are put forward one hour.

TIPPING

In restaurants a *coperto* or cover charge of €1.50–5 is often charged for service and bread. Tipping is not customary in Italy, though a bit extra will be appreciated. For quick service in bars, leave a coin or two with your till receipt when ordering. Taxi drivers do not expect a tip but will appreciate it if you round up the fare to the next euro.

TOILETS

Public toilets are rare. If you use the facilities of cafés and bars, it will be appreciated if you buy a drink.

TOURIST INFORMATION

Italian tourist offices abroad

The website for the UK, North America and Canada Italian tourist offices is www.enit.it.

Canada: 365 Bay Street, Suite 503, Toronto, Ontario, M5H 2V1 tel: 416-925 4882.

UK: 1 Princes Street, London W1B 2AY, tel: 020 7408 1254

US: 686 Park Avenue, New York, NY 10065, tel: 212-245 5618; 401 North Michigan Avenue, Suite 172, Chicago, Illinois 60611, tel: 312-644 9335; 10850 Wilshire Boulevard, Suite 575, Los Angeles, CA 90024, tel: 310-820 1898,

Regional tourist offices

Stresa: Piazza Marconi 16, tel: 0323 30150, www.visitstresa.com.

Como: Piazza Cavour 17, tel: 031 269712, www.lakecomo.org.

Sirmione: Viale Marconi 2, tel: 030 916114, www.sirmionebs.it.

Bergamo: Viale Papa Giovanni XXIII 57, c/o Urban Center, Città Bassa, tel: 035 210204; Via Gombito 13, Città Alta, tel: 035 242226; there is also a very helpful tourist office at Bergamo's Orio al Serio airport, www.visitbergamo.net/en.

Verona: Via degli Alpini 9 (Piazza Brà), tel: 045 8068680, www.tourism.verona.it.
Milan: Piazza Castello 1, tel: 02 80580614, www.turismo.milano.it.

TRANSPORT

By boat. Ferries, hydrofoils and excursion cruisers operate services on all the main lakes. Hydrofoils *(aliscafi)* and catamarans *(catamarani)* are faster than ferries *(battelli)* but are more expensive and have inside seating only. Useful car ferries *(traghetti)* link Intra and Laveno on Lake Maggiore; Menaggio, Varenna, Cadenabbia and Bellagio on Lake Como; and Maderno to Torri del Benaco and Limone to Malcesine on Lake Garda.

Timetables are available from ticket offices, tourist information offices and other outlets, or online at www.navlaghi.it (lakes Maggiore, Como and Garda) or www.navigazionelagoiseo.it (Lake Iseo). Tickets can normally be bought at the point of departure; if bought on board they are a bit more expensive. Ferries normally run from 7am to about 7pm, though in mid-summer the main lakes also offer occasional evening ferry trips with dinner on board.

The ferry companies offer a complex variety of tickets and deals for the major lakes. These include all-day tickets for all or part of a lake, single or return ferry or hydrofoil tickets and ferry tickets which include entry to (or a price reduction at) major attractions. Generally, children under the age of 4 travel free, 4–12s are just over half price, and over 65s from the EU are entitled to a 20 percent reduction on weekdays on the normal ferries *(batelli)*.

By bus. Reasonably priced and fairly regular buses link towns and villages along the lakeshores. Tickets can usually be bought on board for local services, but for urban routes you will need to purchase tickets in advance. These are available from tobacconists and newsstands or at bus stations and must be stamped when you board the bus.

By rail. For mainline train information visit Trenitalia on www.trenitalia.com. Milan is a major rail junction with excellent, reasonably priced services to the main lakes and towns across the region. The lakes themselves, however, are better served by ferries and buses. The cost of rail travel is cheap in comparison to other European countries. The price of a journey depends on the type of train. You can either take the slower services which stop at all the towns or the fast Intercity or Italia Eurostar (ES) trains which levy a supplement of at least 30 percent and require seat reservations. It is advisable to make a reservation well in advance. Many stations now have automatic machines to issue tickets (with instructions in English). Return tickets offer no saving on two singles. Tickets must be stamped in the yellow machines at the near end of the platforms before boarding the train. Tickets bought on the train incur a very hefty supplement.

Taxis. Taxis can be found in main squares in the larger towns. Beware of touts without meters – especially near airports and main train stations. Taxi fares are quite high and there are additional charges, posted in the taxis, for luggage, trips at night and on Sundays and holidays.

V

VISA AND ENTRY REQUIREMENTS

For citizens of EU countries a valid passport or identity card is all that is needed to enter Italy for stays of up to 90 days. Citizens of the US, Canada, Australia and New Zealand require only a valid passport.

Visas *(permesso di soggiorno)*. For stays of more than 90 days a visa is required. Contact your country's Italian Embassy.

Customs. Free exchange of non duty-free goods for personal use is allowed between EU countries. Those from non-EU countries should refer to their home country's regulating organisation for a current complete list of import restrictions.

Currency restrictions. Tourists may bring an unlimited amount of Italian or foreign currency into the country. On departure you must declare any currency beyond the equivalent of €10,000, so it's wise to declare sums exceeding this amount when you arrive.

W

WEBSITES AND INTERNET ACCESS

The official Italian Government Tourist Board site is www.enit.it which has links for the different regions covered by the lakes.

The following are official tourist board sites for the lakes:

www.distrettolaghi.it – Lake Orta and the west of Lake Maggiore.

www.lakecomo.com – Lake Como.

www.visitgarda.com – Lake Garda.

www.visittrentino.it – Trentino.

www.visitbergamo.net – Bergamo.

www.tourism.verona.it – Verona province including the east side of Lake Garda.

www.navlaghi.it – excellent ferry website for the major lakes with timetables and descriptions of destinations.

www.agriturismo.com – details of farm holidays and B&Bs.

For websites of tourist offices in the main towns, see page 130.

Most hotels offer internet access, and an increasing number have Wi-Fi. Charges sometimes apply though in many hotels Wi-Fi is free in public areas and increasingly, in the rooms. Cafés and centres with Wi-Fi services can be hard to come by outside the larger towns. There is usually a nominal fee and if you are using an internet point you will normally be required to produce your passport or ID.

Y

YOUTH HOSTELS

The lakes region only has a dozen or so youth hostels and reservations are essential in summer. An HI (Hostelling International) card is normally required but temporary membership is available at hostels for a small fee. Italian youth hostels are run by the Associazione Italiana Alberghi per la Gioventù (AIG), www.aighostels.com; information is also available through Hostelling International (www.hihostels.com).

RECOMMENDED HOTELS

In high season, hotels with their own restaurant may insist on half board, with stays of no less than three days. Lakeside hotels usually charge a supplement for lake views and it is usually worth paying the extra. Many of the hotels in the lakes close for winter, but those in the cities stay open all year. Booking ahead is recommended in high season.

The symbols below are a rough indication of what you can expect to pay in high season for a twin room with bathroom, including breakfast, taxes and service.

€€€€	**over 350 euros**
€€€	**200–350 euros**
€€	**130–200 euros**
€	**below 130 euros**

LAKE MAGGIORE

Borromeo Islands

Hotel Ristorante Verbano €€ *Isola dei Pescatori, tel: 0323 30408,* www.hotelverbano.it. A delightful alternative to the grand old hotels of Stresa, the Verbano is a 5-minute ferry ride away on the tiny Isola dei Pescatori. The simple pink villa and its restaurant terraces enjoy romantic views of the lake and Isola Bella. The 12 guest rooms, all named after flowers, have parquet floors, handsome antiques and large bathrooms. The island is busy with tourists by day, but delightfully peaceful at night. The hotel provides a free private boat service to Stresa and Baveno at night when the ferry service ends.

Cannero Riviera

Cannero €€ *Piazza Umberto 12, tel: 0323 788046,* www.hotelcannero.com. In a fine lake setting, this is a traditional hotel in what was formerly a monastery and an adjacent private mansion. Family-run and friendly, it provides first-class service and delightful lake and mountain-view guest rooms. Facilities include a sitting room with foreign-language books, an open-air pool, tennis court and restaurant with lakeside terrace.

Cannobio

Cannobio €€ *Piazza Vittorio Emanuele III 6, tel: 0323 739639,* www.hotelcannobio.com. A long-established hotel with a romantic setting on the lakefront by the old harbour. The décor successfully combines the original features of the historic building with contemporary colours and designs. At the Porto Vecchio restaurant (attached to the hotel but under different management), the ravishing lakeside terrace more than compensates for run-of-the-mill cuisine.

Pironi €€ *Via Marconi 35, tel: 0323 70624,* www.pironihotel.it. Twelve comfortable rooms in a beautifully converted medieval Franciscan monastery in the picturesque centre of Cannobio. The three-star hotel is furnished with antiques and retains wonderful original features such as frescoes, vaulted ceilings and old stone columns. The old cellars have been converted into a chic wine bar.

Luino

Camin Hotel Colmegna €€ *Via A. Palazzi 1, Colmegna (3km/2 miles north of Luino), tel: 0332 510855,* www.caminhotel.com. The villa was built on the lake in the early 18th century as part of a hunting estate and retains a large park with romantic trails and a waterfall. Facilities include a private beach, a small stone harbour where motorboats can be rented and lake-side terraces for summer meals. Three apartments are also available.

Stresa

Grand Hotel des Iles Borromées €€€€ *Corso Umberto I, 67, tel: 0323 938938,* www.borromees.it. The grandest hotel on Lake Maggiore, where literary luminaries such as Ernest Hemingway, George Bernard Shaw and John Steinbeck, as well as numerous European royals, have stayed (you can stay in Hemingway's room for €3,000 a night). Sumptuous public rooms are decorated with Murano chandeliers, stucco and antiques; many of the luxurious guest rooms have fabulous views of the Borromeo islands and the Alps. Facilities include one indoor and two outdoor swimming pools, spa club, tennis court, private heliport and landing for private boats.

LAKE COMO

Argegno

Villa Belvedere €€–€€€ *Via Milano 8, tel: 031 821116,* https://villabelvedererelais.com. An alluring villa hotel right on the lake, with glorious views from the terrace where meals are served in summer. Run by the Cappelletti family for 60 years the villa has 20 simply furnished rooms – it's worth paying extra for the ones with lake views. Argegno is a small village with a landing stage close to the hotel for ferry trips of Lake Como.

Bellagio

Florence €€ *Piazza Mazzini 46, tel: 031 950342,* www.hotelflorencebellagio.it. An 18th-century villa (with a later extension) which has been in the same family for over 100 years. The beamed and vaulted foyer combines traditional furnishings with modern colours and innovative works of art. The shady lakeside terrace is an idyllic spot for a drink or summer dining. Comfortable bedrooms in classical style are priced according to views – most look out on to the lake. The spa offers massage, aromatherapy, sauna and jacuzzi.

Grand Hotel Villa Serbelloni €€€€ *Via Roma 1, tel: 031 950216,* www.villaserbelloni.com. Built as a luxury villa on the banks of the lake for an aristocratic Milanese family the villa was converted to a hotel in 1873. Since then it has been hosting royalty, famous politicians and film stars. Grand and opulent public rooms boast crystal chandeliers, stuccowork, marble, gilding and antiques. Guests can take advantage of the spa, tennis courts, swimming pool – and Ettore Bácchia's artfully presented molecular cuisine in the Michelin-starred lakeside restaurant.

Cadenabbia di Griante

Alberghetto della Marianna € *Via Regina 57, tel: 0344 43095,* www.la-marianna.com. A home-from-home bed and breakfast with eight simply-furnished rooms overlooking the lake. Small and friendly, it is run by Paola, who is very hospitable and will help you arrange the day's itinerary. Guests receive a 15 percent discount at La Cucina della Marianna restaurant on the same premises, which offers excellent regional cuisine created by Paola's husband, Ty Valentini.

Cernobbio

Villa d'Este €€€€ *Via Regina 40, tel: 031 3481,* www.villadeste.com. This famous and palatial 16th-century villa in luxuriant gardens on the shores of Lake Como ranks among the best hotels in the world. It was once home to the estranged wife of George IV, and since becoming a hotel the roll call of famous guests has included J.F. Kennedy, Alfred Hitchcock and Madonna. Expect exquisite decor, with antiques and Como silks, and ample facilities including watersports, eight tennis courts, fitness centre, beauty centre, an indoor and a lake-floating swimming pool, and a helipad.

San Fedele D'Intelvi

Villa Simplicitas €€ *San Fedele d'Intelvi (15 mins' drive from Lake Como), tel: 031 831132,* www.villasimplicitas.it. Between lakes Como and Lugano, this 19th-century country house enjoys a peaceful rural setting. Downstairs there's a large open fireplace, an antique billiards table, and a conservatory and terrace for meals. Ten characterful guest rooms are decorated with antiques, curios and wrought-iron and brass beds.

Sotto il Monte

Agriturismo Casa Clelia € *Via Corna 1/3, Sotto il Monte, tel: 035 799133,* www.agriturismocasaclelia.it. This wonderfully peaceful retreat, 20km (12 miles) west of Bergamo, dates back to the 11th century in the days when it was a convent. Thanks to a creative and ecological restoration, it is now a working farm with surrounding woodlands, gardens and farm animals. The ten spacious and stylish guest rooms have wooden floors, beamed ceilings and polished antiques. The stonewalled rustic dining room with log fire or the wisteria and jasmine clad arbour in summer are the setting for excellent and affordable cuisine, with many ingredients straight from the farm.

Varenna

Albergo Milano €€ *Via XX Settembre 35, tel: 0341 830298,* www.varenna.net. A gem of a hotel in the centre of picturesque Varenna. There are only 12 rooms (book well in advance), all individually furnished, with balconies and lake views. There are also a couple of apartments with a kitchenette in the new annexes. The inviting La Vista restaurant has a terrace with gorgeous lake views.

Albergo Olivedo €€ *Piazza Martiri della Libertà 14, tel: 0341 830115,* www.olivedo.it. This Art Nouveau villa lies across from the ferry dock at Varenna so while it's not as peaceful as some lakeside hotels it's ideal for hops across to Bellagio or Menaggio. Most of the guest rooms (and all five in neighbouring Villa Torretta, under the same ownership) have wonderful views of the lake. The Olivedo restaurant, with reasonable prices and top-notch home-made ravioli, is a great spot for watching the world go by.

LAKE GARDA

Gardone Riviera

Grand Hotel Fasano €€€ *Corso Zanardelli 190, tel: 0365 290220,* www.ghf.it. A converted 19th-century hunting lodge, this 5-star hotel has extensive gardens, new luxury spa and a variety of rooms and views, priced accordingly. The separate Villa Principe on the lake offers water sports, a tennis court, golf and a lakeside restaurant.

Villa Fiordaliso €€€€ *Corso Zanardelli 150, tel: 0365 20158,* www.villafiordaliso.it. Exclusive Art Nouveau villa where Mussolini and Clara

Petacci stayed before they were caught and executed in 1945 (see page 23). The hotel is on a busy road but there are gardens leading down to the lake and the Michelin-starred restaurant (one of the best on Lake Garda) has a romantic lakeside setting. There are just seven rooms: six doubles and the pricey Clara Petacci suite.

Gargnano

Gardenia al Lago €€€ *Via Colletta 53, Villa di Gargnano, tel: 0365 71195,* www.hotel-gardenia.it. Enchanting villa hotel with gardens down to the lake. The welcoming Arosio family have run the hotel for over half a century; guest rooms are traditional with antiques and tiled floors, each with terrace or balcony. Weather permitting, you can breakfast by the water's edge, in the shade of olive and bay trees.

Hotel du Lac €€ *Via Colletta 21, Villa di Gargnano, tel: 0365 71107,* www.hotel-dulac.it. Sister hotel of the Gardenia, the Hotel du Lac has a heavenly setting, with the same lovely views and family-run atmosphere. Charmingly old fashioned, with handsome antiques in the bedrooms; the restaurant, with summer terrace, overhangs the lake.

Riva del Garda

Locanda Restel de Fer € *Via Restel de Fer 10, tel: 0464 553481,* www.resteldefer.com. The Meneghelli family, who have been here since 1400, run a highly regarded restaurant (see page 110) and offer five simple guest rooms, and more modern apartments in a new building which can accommodate 2–4 guests. Three nights minimum stay.

Sirmione

Meublé Grifone € *Via Gaetano Bocchio 4, tel: 030 916014,* www.sirmionehotelgrifone.it. One of the few cheaper options in Sirmione, and romantically located right by the castle, the Grifone books up fast. It is a very simple hotel with 16 basic rooms, the best of which have balconies over the lake.

Villa Cortine €€€€ *Viale C. Gennari 2, tel: 030 9905890,* www.palace hotelvillacortine.com. Opulent and exclusive villa, built in 1870, with a 20th-century wing added to convert it into a hotel. Away from the bustling centre of Sirmione, the hotel enjoys an enticing setting within 4.8 hectares (12 acres) of parkland leading down to the lakeshore. Half board is compulsory in season. Facilities include a jetty with boats to hire, heated and outdoor swimming pool and tennis courts; water sports can be arranged.

Torri del Benaco

Gardesana €€ *Piazza Calderini 5, tel: 045 7225411,* www.hotel-garde sana.com. Historic hotel with a very congenial atmosphere, a nice restaurant (see page 110) and comfortable, reasonably priced rooms overlooking the harbour and castle. Royalty, politicians and film stars have stayed here, among them Churchill, Vivien Leigh, Lawrence Olivier and Maria Callas.

LAKE ISEO

I Due Roccoli €€€ *Colline di Iseo, tel: 030 9822977,* www.idueroc coli.com. Charming villa hotel in the hills above the town of Iseo. Half board is to be recommended given the quality of the cuisine, the local Franciacorta wines and the fabulous lake views from the candlelit courtyard. The seductive setting appeals to honeymooners looking for a peaceful retreat away from the busy lake resorts. Facilities include an outdoor pool and tennis court.

LAKE ORTA

Orta San Giulio

Aracoeli €€ *Piazza Motta 34, tel: 0322 905173,* www.ortainfo.com. A hotel with an enchanting location on the main square, with romantic views of the lake and island. The décor is a mix of wood-beamed ceilings and stone walls and contemporary design. However, it has seen better years.

Villa Crespi €€€€ *Via Fava 18, tel: 0322 911902,* www.villacrespi.it. Opulent Moorish villa dominated by a lofty minaret within parkland near the lake. Charmed by his visit to Baghdad, Cristoforo Benigno Crespi built the villa in 1879. It is now a 4-star hotel, run by a Neapolitan and his wife, offering luxury guest rooms with marble bathrooms (six doubles, eight suites), fitness room, shiatsu and a gourmet restaurant with two Michelin stars (see page 111).

Pettenasco

L'Approdo €€ *Corso Roma 80, Pettenasco, tel: 0323 89345,* www.lagodortahotels.com. On the lakeshore at the small village of Pettenasco, just north of Orta San Giulio, this modern hotel would suit any sports enthusiast. You can windsurf, water-ski, canoe, rent boats, play tennis, swim from the beach or do leisurely lengths in the 25-metre heated outdoor pool. Most of the 72 balconied guest rooms overlook the lake; others look out on to the garden.

CITY HOTELS

Bergamo

B&B Bergamo Alta € *Via San Lorenzo 24, tel: 334 1099335,* www.bergamoaltabb.it. Located in a centuries old building in the historical centre of the Città Alta (the upper town), this is a pleasant family-run spot with a good breakfast. There are views from the property over the surrounding countryside. Many of the city's main sights are minutes away on foot.

Gombit Hotel €€ *Via Mario Lupo 6, tel: 035 247009;* www.gombithotel.it. Opened in 2010 next to the 13th century Torre del Gombito, this was the first designer hotel in the Città Alta. Modern and stylish, the 13 guest rooms are individually decorated, typically with exposed brick stonework or timbers, warm wood floors, pastel-coloured furnishings and chic modern bathrooms. There is no restaurant but Bergamo is full of gastronomic delights and there are excellent places to eat within a stone's throw.

Verona

Due Torri Hotel Baglioni €€€€ *Piazza Sant'Anastasia 4, tel: 045 595044,* https://hotelduetorri.duetorrihotels.com. Luxury hotel in imposing 14th-century villa, beside the church of Sant'Anastasia. Public rooms are grandiose, with antiques, vaulted ceilings and frescoes. Guest rooms are old-fashioned in style but well-equipped. This is a favourite location of opera stars.

Torcolo €€ *Vicolo Listone 3, tel: 045 8007512,* www.hoteltorcolo.it. Small, homely and appealing 2-star hotel very close to the Arena and popular with opera fans who book their favourite room months in advance of the season. Comfortable guest rooms are individually furnished, all in an attractive traditional style. Out of the opera season breakfasts are not included in the room rate, so you may choose instead to have coffee and croissants on Piazza Brà overlooking the Arena.

DICTIONARY

ENGLISH–ITALIAN

adj adjective **adv** adverb **BE** British English **n** noun **prep** preposition **v** verb

A

a.m. del mattino
abbey l'abbazia
accept *v* accettare
access l'accesso
accident l'incidente
accommodation l'alloggio
account il conto
acupuncture l'agopuntura
adapter l'adattatore
address l'indirizzo
admission l'ingresso
after dopo; **~noon** il pomeriggio; **~shave** il dopobarba
age l'età
agency l'agenzia
AIDS l'AIDS
air l'aria; **~ conditioning** l'aria condizionata; **~ pump** la pompa dell'aria; **~line** la compagnia aerea; **~mail** la posta aerea; **~plane** l'aereo; **~port** l'aeroporto
aisle il corridoio; **~ seat** il posto sul corridoio
allergic allergico; **~ reaction** la reazione allergica
allow *v* permettere
alone solo
alter *v* modificare
alternate route il percorso alternativo
aluminum foil la carta stagnola
amazing straordinario
ambulance l'ambulanza
American americano
amusement park il lunapark
and and
anemic anemico
anesthesia l'anestesia
animal l'animale
ankle la caviglia
antibiotic l'antibiotico
antiques store il negozio d'antiquariato
antiseptic cream la crema antisettica
anything qualsiasi cosa
apartment l'appartamento
appendix (body part) l'appendice
appetizer l'antipasto
appointment l'appuntamento
arcade la sala giochi
area code il prefisso
arm il braccio
aromatherapy l'aromaterapia
around (the corner) dietro di
arrivals (airport) gli arrivi
arrive *v* arrivare
artery l'arteria
arthritis l'artrite
art l'arte
aspirin l'aspirina
asthmatic asmatico
ATM il bancomat
attack l'aggressione
attend *v* frequentare
attraction (place) l'attrattiva
attractive attraente
Australia Australia
Australian australiano
automatic automatico; **~ car** l'auto col cambio automatico
available libero

B

baby il bebè; **~ bottle** il biberon; **~ wipe** la salvietta per neonati; **~sitter** la babysitter
back (body part) la schiena; **~ache** il mal di schiena; **~pack** lo zaino
bag la borsa
baggage il bagaglio; **~ claim** il ritiro bagagli; **~ ticket** lo scontrino bagagli
bakery la panetteria
ballet lo spettacolo di danza
bandage la benda
bank la banca
bar il bar
barbecue il barbecue
barber il barbiere
baseball il baseball
basket (grocery store) il cestino
basketball il basketball
bathroom il bagno
battery la batteria
battleground il campo di battaglia
be *v* essere
beach la spiaggia
beautiful bello
bed il letto; **~ and breakfast** la pensione
begin *v* iniziare
before prima

beginner il principiante
behind dietro
beige beige
belt la cintura
berth la cuccetta
best il migliore
better migliore
bicycle la bicicletta
big grande
bigger più grande
bike route il percorso ciclabile
bikini il bikini; **~ wax** la ceretta all'inguine
bill *v* **(charge)** fatturare; **~** *n* **(money)** la banconota; **~** *n* **(of sale)** il conto
bird l'uccello
birthday il compleanno
black nero
bladder la vescica
bland insipido
blanket la coperta
bleed *v* sanguinare
blood il sangue; **~ pressure** la pressione sanguigna
blouse la camicetta
blue blu
board *v* imbarcarsi
boarding pass la carta d'imbarco
boat la barca
bone l'osso
book il libro; **~store** la libreria
boots gli stivali
boring noioso
botanical garden il giardino botanico
bother *v* infastidire
bottle la bottiglia; **~ opener** l'apribottiglie
bowl la coppa
box la scatola
boxing match l'incontro di boxe
boy il ragazzo; **~friend** il ragazzo
bra il reggiseno
bracelet il braccialetto
brakes (car) i freni
break *v* rompere; **~-in (burglary)** il furto con scasso; **~down** il guasto
breakfast la colazione
breast il petto; **~feed** *v* allattare
breathe *v* respirare
bridge il ponte
briefs (clothing) lo slip
bring *v* portare
British britannico(a)
broken rotto
brooch la spilla
broom la scopa
brother il fratello
brown marrone
bug l'insetto
building l'edificio
burn *v* bruciare
bus l'autobus; **~ station** la stazione degli autobus; **~ stop** la fermata del bus; **~ ticket** il biglietto del bus; **~ tour** l'escursione in pullman
business il lavoro; **~ card** il biglietto da visita; **~ center** il centro business; **~ class** la classe business; **~ hours** l'orario d'apertura
butcher il macellaio
buttocks le natiche
buy *v* comprare
bye ciao

C

cabaret il cabaret
cabin la cabina
cable car la funivia
cafe il caffè
call *v* chiamare; **~** *n* la chiamata
calories le calorie
camera la macchina fotografica; **digital ~** la macchina fotografica digitale; **~ case** l'astuccio della macchina fotografica; **~ store** il negozio di fotografia
camp *v* campeggiare; **~ stove** il fornello da campeggio; **~site** il campeggio
can opener l'apriscatole
Canada il Canada
Canadian canadese
cancel *v* annullare
candy le caramelle
canned good lo scatolame
canyon il canalone
car l'auto; **~ hire [BE]** l'autonoleggio; **~ park [BE]** il parcheggio; **~ rental** l'autonoleggio; **~ seat** il seggiolino per auto
carafe la caraffa
card la carta; **ATM ~** il bancomat; **credit ~** la carta di credito; **debit ~** il bancomat; **phone ~** la scheda telefonica
carry on board *v* **[BE]** portare a bordo
carry-on il bagaglio a mano
cart (grocery store) il carrello; **~ (luggage)** il carrello
carton il cartone; **~ of cigarettes** la stecca di sigarette
case (container) la cassa
cash *v* incassare; **~** *n* i contanti; **~ advance** l'acconto
cashier il cassiere
casino il casinò
castle il castello
cathedral la cattedrale
cave la grotta
CD il CD
cell phone il telefonino
Celsius Celsius
centimeter il centimetro
certificate il certificato

chair la sedia; **~ lift** la seggiovia
change *v* **(buses)** cambiare; **~** *v* **(money)** cambiare; **~** *v* **(baby)** cambiare; **~** *n* **(money)** il cambio
charcoal il carbone
charge *v* **(credit card)** addebitare; **~** *n* **(cost)** il costo
cheap economico; **~er** più economico
check *v* **(on something)** controllare; **~** *v* **(luggage)** controllare; **~** *n* **(payment)** l'assegno; **~-in (hotel/airport)** il check-in; **~ing account** il conto corrente; **~-out (hotel)** il pagamento del conto
Cheers! Salute!
chemical toilet il WC da campeggio
chemist [BE] la farmacia
cheque [BE] l'assegno
chest (body part) il petto; **~ pain** il dolore al petto
chewing gum la gomma da masticare
child il bambino; **~ seat** il seggiolone; **~'s menu** il menù per bambino; **~'s portion** la porzione per bambino
Chinese cinese
chopsticks i bastoncini cinesi
church la chiesa
cigar il sigaro
cigarette la sigaretta
class la classe; **business ~** la classe business; **economy ~** la classe economica; **first ~** la prima classe
classical music la musica classica
clean *v* pulire; **~** *adj* pulito; **~ing product** il prodotto per la pulizia; **~ing supplies** i prodotti per la pulizia
clear *v* **(on an ATM)** cancellare
cliff la scogliera
cling film [BE] la pellicola per alimenti
close *v* **(a shop)** chiudere
close vicino
closed chiuso
clothing l'abbigliamento; **~ store** il negozio d'abbigliamento
club il club
coat il cappotto
coffee shop il caffè
coin la moneta
colander la scolapasta
cold (sickness) il raffreddore; **~ (temperature)** freddo
colleague il collega
cologne la colonia
color il colore
comb il pettine
come *v* venire
complaint il reclamo
computer il computer
concert il concerto; **~ hall** la sala da concerti
condition (medical) la condizione
conditioner il balsamo
condom il preservativo
conference la conferenza
confirm *v* confermare
congestion la congestione
connect *v* **(internet)** collegarsi
connection (internet) il collegamento; **~ (flight)** la coincidenza
constipated costipato
consulate il consolato
consultant il consulente
contact *v* contattare; **~ lens** la lente a contatto; **~ lens solution** la soluzione per lenti a contatto
contagious contagioso
convention hall la sala congressi
conveyor belt il nastro trasportatore
cook *v* cucinare
cooking gas il gas per cucina
cool (temperature) fresco
copper il rame
corkscrew il cavatappi
cost *v* costare
cot il lettino
cotton il cotone
cough *v* tossire; **~** *n* la tosse
country code il prefisso del paese
cover charge il coperto
crash *v* **(car)** fare un incidente
cream (ointment) la crema
credit card la carta di credito
crew neck a girocollo
crib la culla
crystal il cristallo
cup la tazza
currency la valuta; **~ exchange** il cambio valuta; **~ exchange office** l'ufficio di cambio
current account [BE] il conto corrente
customs la dogana
cut v (hair) tagliare; **~** *n* **(injury)** il taglio
cute carino
cycling il ciclismo

D

damage *v* danneggiare; **~d** danneggiato
dance *v* ballare; **~ club** il club di ballo; **~ing** il ballo

dangerous pericoloso
dark scuro
date (calendar) la data
day il giorno
deaf sordo
debit card il bancomat
deck chair la sedia a sdraio
declare *v* dichiarare
decline *v* **(credit card)** rifiutare
deeply profondamente
degrees (temperature) i gradi
delay *v* ritardare
delete *v* **(computer)** eliminare
delicatessen la gastronomia
delicious squisito
denim i jeans
dentist il dentista
denture la dentiera
deodorant il deodorante
department store il grande magazzino
departures (airport) le partenze
deposit *v* depositare; ~ **(bank)** *n* il deposito; ~ **(to reserve a room)** il deposito
desert il deserto
detergent il detersivo
develop *v* **(film)** sviluppare
diabetic diabetico
dial *v* comporre il numero
diamond il diamante
diaper il pannolino
diarrhea la diarrea
diesel il diesel
difficult difficile
digital digitale; ~ **camera** la macchina fotografica digitale; ~ **photos** le foto digitali; ~ **prints** le stampe digitali
dining room la sala da pranzo
dinner la cena
direction la direzione
dirty sporco
disabled il disabile; ~ **accessible [BE]** accessibile ai disabili
disconnect *v (computer)* scollegare
discount lo sconto
dish (kitchen) il piatto; **~washer** la lavastoviglie; **~washing liquid** il detersivo per i piatti
display lo schermo; ~ **case** la vetrinetta
disposable usa e getta; ~ **razor** la lametta usa e getta
dive *v* tuffarsi; **~ing equipment** l'attrezzatura subacquea
divorce *v* divorziare
dizzy stordito
doctor il medico
doll la bambola
dollar (U.S.) il dollaro
domestic domestico; ~ **flight** il volo nazionale
door la porta
dormitory il dormitorio
double bed il letto matrimoniale
downtown (direction) il centro; ~ **area** il centro
dozen la dozzina
drag lift lo ski lift
dress (piece of clothing) il vestito; ~ **code** il codice di abbigliamento
drink *v* bere; ~ *n* la bevanda; ~ **menu** il menù delle bevande; **~ing water** l'acqua potabile
drive *v* guidare
driver's license number il numero di patente
drop (medicine) la goccia
drowsiness la sonnolenza
dry cleaner il lavasecco
dubbed doppiato
during durante
duty (tax) la tassa; ~ **free** duty free
DVD il DVD

E

ear l'orecchio; **~ache** il mal d'orecchio
earlier prima
early presto
earrings gli orecchini
east est
easy facile
eat *v* mangiare
economy class la classe economica
elbow il gomito
electric outlet la presa elettrica
elevator l'ascensore
e-mail *v* inviare e-mail; ~ *n* l'e-mail; ~ **address** l'indirizzo e-mail
emergency l'emergenza; ~ **exit** l'uscita d'emergenza
empty *v* svuotare
enamel (jewelry) lo smalto
end *v* finire
English inglese
engrave *v* incidere
enjoy *v* godersi
enter *v* entrare
entertainment l'intrattenimento
entrance l'entrata
envelope la busta
equipment l'attrezzatura
escalators le scale mobili
estate car [BE] la station wagon

e-ticket il biglietto elettronico
EU resident il residente UE
euro l'euro
evening la sera
excess l'eccesso
exchange v (money) cambiare; ~ *n* **(place)** il cambio; **~ rate** il tasso di cambio
excursion l'escursione
excuse *v* scusare
exhausted esausto
exit *v* uscire; ~ *n* l'uscita
expensive caro
expert esperto
exposure (film) la posa
express espresso; ~ **bus** il bus espresso; **~ train** il treno espresso
extension (phone) l'interno
extra extra; **~ large** extra large
extract *v* **(tooth)** estrarre
eye l'occhio
eyebrow wax la ceretta per sopracciglie

F

face il viso
facial la pulizia del viso
family la famiglia
fan (appliance) il ventilatore; ~ **(souvenir)** il ventaglio
far lontano; **~-sighted** ipermetrope
farm la fattoria
fast veloce; **~ food** il fast food
faster più veloce
fat free senza grassi
father il padre
fax *v* inviare per fax; ~ *n* il fax; **~ number** il numero di fax
fee la tariffa
feed *v* dare da mangiare
ferry il traghetto
fever la febbre
field (sports) il campo
fill *v* riempire; **~ out** *v* **(form)** compilare; **~ing (tooth)** l'otturazione
film (camera) il rullino
fine (fee for breaking law) la multa
finger il dito; **~nail** l'unghia
fire il fuoco; ~ **department** i vigili del fuoco; **~ door** la porta antincendio
first primo; **~ class** la prima classe
fit (clothing) *v* andare bene
fitting room il camerino
fix *v* **(repair)** riparare
flashlight la torcia elettrica
flat tire la gomma a terra
flight il volo
floor il pavimento
flower il fiore
folk music la musica folk
food il cibo
foot il piede
football game [BE] la partita di football
for per
forecast la previsione
forest il bosco
fork la forchetta
form il modulo
formula (baby) il latte in polvere
fort la fortezza
fountain la fontana
free libero
freezer il freezer
fresh fresco
friend l'amico
frying pan la padella
full-service il servizio completo
full-time a tempo pieno

G

game la partita
garage il garage
garbage bag il sacchetto per la spazzatura
gas (cooking) il gas per cucina; ~ **(heating)** il gas; **~ station** la stazione del servizio; ~ **(vehicle)** la benzina
gate (airport) l'uscita
gay gay; **~ bar** il bar per gay; **~ club** il club per gay
gel (hair) il gel
get off *v* **(a train/bus/subway)** scendere
get to *v* arrivare
gift il regalo; **~ shop** il negozio di articoli da regalo
girl la ragazza; **~friend** la ragazza
give *v* dare
glass (drinking) il bicchiere; **~ (material)** il vetro; **~es** gli occhiali
go *v* **(somewhere)** andare
gold l'oro
golf golf; **~ course** il campo da golf; **~ club** la mazza; **~ tournament** la gara di golf
good *n* il bene; ~ *adj* buono; **~ afternoon** buon pomeriggio; **~ evening** buonasera; **~ morning** buongiorno; **~ bye** arrivederla; **~s** le merci
gram il grammo
grandchild il nipote
grandparent il nonno
gray grigio
green verde
grocery store il fruttivendolo
ground floor il pianterreno

groundcloth [groundsheet BE] il telone impermeabile
group il gruppo
guide la guida; ~ **book** la guida; ~ **dog** il cane da guida
gym la palestra
gynecologist il ginecologo

H

hair i capelli; ~ **dryer** l'asciugacapelli; ~ **salon** il parrucchiere; ~**brush** la spazzola ; ~ **cut** il taglio; ~**spray** la lacca; ~**style** l'acconciatura; ~**stylist** il parrucchiere
half la metà; ~ **hour** la mezz'ora; ~-**kilo** il mezzo chilo
hammer il martello
hand la mano; ~ **luggage** il bagaglio a mano; ~**bag** la borsetta
handicapped il disabile; ~ **accessible** accessibile ai disabili
hangover la sbornia
happy felice
hat il cappello
have *v* avere
head (body part) la testa; ~**ache** il mal di testa; ~**phones** gli auricolari
health la salute; ~ **food store** l'erboristeria
heart il cuore; ~ **condition** il disturbo cardiaco
heat il calore; ~**er** il radiatore
hello salve
helmet il casco
help *v* aiutare; ~ *n* l'aiuto
here qui
heterosexual eterosessuale
hi ciao
high alto; ~**chair** il seggiolone; ~-**heeled shoes** le scarpe col tacco alto; ~**way** l'autostrada
hiking boots gli scarponi da montagna
hill la collina
hire *v* **[BE]** noleggiare; ~ **car [BE]** l'auto a noleggio
hitchhike *v* fare l'autostop
hockey l'hockey
holiday [BE] la vacanza
horse track l'ippodromo
hospital l'ospedale
hostel l'ostello
hot (temperature) caldo; ~ **(spicy)** piccante; ~ **springs** le terme; ~ **water** l'acqua calda
hotel l'hotel
hour l'ora
house la casa; ~**hold goods** gli articoli casalinghi; ~**keeping services** i servizi di pulizia domestica
how come; ~ **much** quanto
hug *v* abbracciare
hungry affamato
hurt il dolore
husband il marito

I

ibuprofen l'ibuprofene
ice il ghiaccio; ~ **hockey** l'hockey su ghiaccio
icy gelato
identification l'identificazione
ill malato
in in
include *v* includere
indoor pool la piscina interna
inexpensive a buon mercato
infected infetto
information (phone) le informazioni; ~ **desk** l'ufficio informazioni
insect insetto; ~ **bite** la puntura d'insetto; ~ **repellent** il repellente per gli insetti
insert *v* inserire
insomnia l'insonnia
instant message il messaggio istantaneo
insulin l'insulina
insurance l'assicurazione; ~ **card** la tessera dell'assicurazione; ~ **company** la compagnia di assicurazione
interesting interessante
intermediate intermedio
international (airport area) internazionale; ~ **flight** il volo internazionale; ~ **student card** la tessera internazionale dello studente
internet l'Internet; ~ **cafe** l'Internet caffè; ~ **service** il servizio Internet; **wireless** ~ il collegamento wireless a Internet
interpreter l'interprete
intersection l'incrocio
intestine l'intestino
introduce *v* presentare
invoice [BE] la fattura
Ireland l'Irlanda
Irish irlandese
iron *v* stirare; ~ *n* **(clothes)** il ferro da stiro
Italian italiano
Italy l'Italia

J

jacket la giacca
jar il vaso
jaw la mascella
jazz il jazz; ~ **club** il club jazz
jeans i jeans

jet ski l'acquascooter
jeweler il gioielliere
jewelry la gioielleria
join *v* unire
joint (body part) la giuntura

K

key la chiave; **~ card** la chiave elettronica; **~ ring** il portachiavi
kiddie pool la piscina per bambini
kidney (body part) il rene
kilo il chilo; **~gram** il chilogrammo; **~meter** il chilometro
kiss *v* baciare
kitchen la cucina; **~ foil** la carta stagnola
knee il ginocchio
knife il coltello

L

lace il pizzo
lactose intolerant intollerante al lattosio
lake il lago
large grande
larger più grande
last ultimo
late (time) tardi
later più tardi
launderette [BE] la lavanderia a gettone
laundromat la lavanderia a gettone
laundry la lavanderia; **~ facility** il locale lavanderia; **~ service** il servizio di lavanderia
lawyer l'avvocato
leather la pelle
leave *v* partire
left (direction) a sinistra
leg la gamba
lens la lente
less meno
lesson la lezione
letter la lettera
library la biblioteca
life la vita; **~ jacket** il giubbotto di salvataggio; **~guard** il bagnino
lift (ride) il passaggio; **~ [BE]** l'ascensore; **~ pass** il lift pass
light (overhead) la lampada; **~** *v* **(cigarette)** accendere; **~bulb** la lampadina; **~er** l'accendino
like *v* **(someone)** piacere
line (train) la linea
linen il lino
lip il labbro
liquor store l'enoteca
liter il litro
little piccolo
live *v* vivere
liver (body part) il fegato
loafers i mocassini
local locale
lock *v* chiudere; **~** *n* la serratura
locker l'armadietto
log off *v* **(computer)** fare il logoff
log on *v* **(computer)** fare il logon
long lungo; **~ sleeves** le maniche lunghe; **~-sighted [BE]** ipermetrope
look *v* guardare
lose *v* **(something)** perdere
lost perso; **~ and found** l'ufficio oggetti smarriti
lotion la lozione
louder più forte
love *v* **(someone)** amare; **~** *n* l'amore
low basso; **~er** più basso
luggage il bagaglio; **~ cart** il carrello bagagli; **~ locker** l'armadietto dei bagagli; **~ ticket** lo scontrino dei bagagli; **hand ~ [BE]** il bagaglio a mano
lunch il pranzo
lung il polmone

M

magazine la rivista
magnificent magnifico
mail *v* spedire; **~** *n* la posta; **~box** la cassetta della posta
main principale; **~ attraction** l'attrattiva principale; **~ course** il piatto principale
make up [BE] (a prescription) il trucco
mall il centro commerciale
man l'uomo
manager il responsabile
manicure il manicure
manual car l'auto col cambio manuale
map la cartina
market il mercato
married sposato
marry *v* sposare
mass (church service) la messa
massage il massaggio
match *n* **(wooden stick)** il fiammifero; **~** *n* **(game)** la partita
meal il pasto
measure *v* **(someone/something)** misurare; **~ing cup** la tazza di misurazione; **~ing spoon** il misurino
mechanic il meccanico
medicine la medicina
medium (size) medio
meet *v* **(someone)** incontrare
meeting (corporate) la riunione; **~ room** sala riunioni
membership card la tessera associativa
memorial (place) il monumento
memory card la scheda memoria

mend *v* riparare
menstrual cramp il crampo mestruale
menu il menù
message il messaggio
meter (parking) il parchimetro
microwave il microonde
midday [BE] mezzogiorno
midnight mezzanotte
mileage il chilometraggio
mini-bar il minibar
minute il minuto
missing (was never there) mancante; scomparso **(was previously there)**
mistake l'errore
mobile mobile; **~ home** la casa prefabbricata; **~ phone [BE]** il telefonino
mobility la mobilità
money il denaro
month il mese
mop lo spazzolone
moped lo scooter
more più
morning il mattino
mosque la moschea
mother la madre
motor il motore; **~ boat** il motoscafo; **~cycle** la motocicletta; **~way [BE]** l'autostrada
mountain la montagna; **~ bike** la mountain bike
mousse (hair) la mousse
mouth la bocca
movie il film; **~ theater** il cinema
mug *v* scippare
muscle il muscolo
museum il museo
music la musica; **~ store** il negozio di musica

N

nail l'unghia; **~ file** la lima; **~ salon** il salone di bellezza
name il nome
napkin il tovagliolo
nappy [BE] il pannolino
nationality la nazionalità
nature preserve la riserva naturale
(be) nauseous *v* avere la nausea
near vicino; **~-sighted** miope
neck il collo; **~lace** la collana
need *v* necessitare
newspaper il giornale
newsstand l'edicola
next prossimo
nice sympatico
night la notte; **~club** il nightclub
no no
non-alcoholic analcolico
non-smoking non fumatori
noon mezzogiorno
north nord
nose il naso
notes [BE] le banconote
nothing niente
notify *v* avvertire
novice il principiante
now ora
number il numero
nurse l'infermiere

O

office l'ufficio; **~ hours** l'orario d'ufficio
off-licence [BE] l'enoteca
oil l'olio
OK OK
old vecchio
on the corner all'angolo
once una volta
one uno; **~-way (ticket)** solo andata; **~-way street** il senso unico
only solo
open *v* aprire; **~** *adj* aperto
opera l'opera; **~ house** il teatro dell'opera
opposite di fronte a
optician l'ottico
orange (color) arancione
orchestra l'orchestra
order *v* ordinare
outdoor pool la piscina esterna
outside fuori
over sopra; **~ the counter (medication)** da banco; **~look (scenic place)** il belvedere; **~night** per la notte
oxygen treatment l'ossigeno terapia

P

p.m. del pomeriggio
pacifier il ciuccio
pack *v* fare le valigie
package il pacchetto
paddling pool [BE] la piscina per bambini
pad [BE] l'assorbente
pain il dolore
pajamas il pigiama
palace il palazzo
pants i pantaloni
pantyhose il collant
paper la carta; **~ towel** la carta da cucina
paracetamol [BE] il paracetamolo
park *v* parcheggiare; **~** *n* il parco; **~ing garage** il parcheggio; **~ing lot** il parcheggio
parliament building l'edificio del parlamento
part (for car) il ricambio; **~ time** part-time
pass through *v* passare
passenger il passeggero

passport il passaporto; **~ control** il controllo passaporti
password la password
pastry shop la pasticceria
path il sentiero
pay *v* pagare; **~ phone** il telefono pubblico
peak (of a mountain) la vetta
pearl la perla
pedestrian il pedone
pediatrician il pediatra
pedicure il pedicure
pen la penna
penicillin la penicillina
per per; **~ day** al giorno; **~ hour** all'ora; **~ night** a notte; **~ week** a settimana
perfume il profumo
period (menstrual) il ciclo; **~ (of time)** il periodo
permit *v* permettere
petite piccolo
petrol [BE] la benzina; **~ station [BE]** la stazione di servizio
pewter il peltro
pharmacy la farmacia
phone *v* telefonare; **~** *n* il telefono; **~ call** la telefonata; **~ card** la scheda telefonica; **~ number** il numero di telefono
photo la foto; **~copy** la fotocopia; **~graphy** la fotografia
pick up *v* **(something)** raccogliere
picnic area la zona picnic
piece il pezzo
Pill (birth control) la pillola
pillow il cuscino
personal identification number (PIN) il codice PIN
pink rosa
piste [BE] la pista; **~ map [BE]** la cartina delle piste
pizzeria la pizzeria
place a bet *v* scommettere
plane l'aereo
plastic wrap la pellicola per alimenti
plate il piatto
platform (train) il binario
platinum il platino
play *v* giocare; **~** *n* **(theater)** lo spettacolo; **~ ground** il parco giochi; **~ pen** il box
please per favore
pleasure il piacere
plunger lo sturalavandini
plus size la taglia forte
pocket la tasca
poison il veleno
poles (skiing) le racchette
police la polizia; **~ report** il verbale di polizia; **~ station** il commissariato
pond lo stagno
pool (swimming) la piscina
pop music la musica pop
portion la porzione
post [BE] la posta; **~ office** l'ufficio postale; **~box [BE]** la buca delle lettere; **~card** la cartolina
pot (for cooking) la pentola; **~ (for flowers)** il vaso
pottery la ceramica
pounds (British sterling) le sterline
pregnant incinta
prescribe *v* prescrivere
prescription la ricetta
press *v* **(clothing)** stirare
price il prezzo
print *v* stampare
problem il problema
produce la frutta e verdura; **~ store** il fruttivendolo
prohibit *v* proibire
pronounce *v* pronunciare
public pubblico
pull *v* **(door sign)** tirare
purple viola
purse la borsetta
push *v* **(door sign)** spingere; **~chair [BE]** il passeggino

Q

quality la qualità
question la domanda
quiet tranquillo

R

racetrack il circuito
racket (sports) la racchetta
railway station [BE] la stazione ferroviaria
rain la pioggia; **~coat** l'impermeabile; **~forest** la foresta pluviale; **~y** piovoso
rape *v* stuprare; **~** *n* lo stupro
rash l'irritazione
razor blade la lametta
reach *v* raggiungere
ready pronto
real vero
receipt la ricevuta
receive *v* ricevere
reception la reception
recharge *v* ricaricare
recommend *v* raccomandare
recommendation la raccomandazione
recycling il reciclaggio
red rosso
refrigerator il frigorifero
region la regione
registered mail la raccomandata
regular normale
relationship la relazione

rent *v* affittare
rental car l'auto a noleggio
repair *v* riparare
repeat *v* ripetere
reservation la prenotazione; ~ **desk** l'ufficio prenotazioni
reserve *v* prenotare
restaurant il ristorante
restroom la toilette
retired in pensione
return *v* **(something)** portare indietro; ~ *n* **[BE]** la resa
rib (body part) la costola
right (direction) a destra; ~ **of way** la precedenza
ring l'anello
river il fiume
road map la cartina stradale
rob *v* rubare; **~bed** derubato
romantic romantico
room la stanza; ~ **key** la chiave della stanza; ~ **service** il servizio in camera
round-trip l'andata e ritorno
route il percorso
rowboat la barca a remi
rubbish [BE] la spazzatura; ~ **bag [BE]** il sacchetto per la spazzatura
rugby il rugby
ruins le rovine
rush la fretta

S

sad triste
safe (receptacle) la cassaforte; ~ **(protected)** sicuro
sales tax l'IVA
same stesso
sandals i sandali
sanitary napkin l'assorbente
saucepan la pentola
sauna la sauna
save *v* **(computer)** salvare
savings (account) i risparmi
scanner lo scanner
scarf la sciarpa
schedule *v* programmare; ~ *n* il programma
school la scuola
science la scienza
scissors le forbici
sea il mare
seat il posto
security la sicurezza
see *v* vedere
self-service il self-service
sell *v* vendere
seminar il seminario
send *v* inviare
senior citizen l'anziano
separated (marriage) separato
serious serio
service (in a restaurant) il servizio
sexually transmitted disease (STD) la malattia sessualmente trasmissibile
shampoo lo shampoo
sharp appuntito
shaving cream la crema da barba
sheet (bedlinen) il lenzuolo; ~ **(paper)** la pagina
ship *v* **(mail)** inviare
shirt la camicia
shoes le scarpe; ~ **store** il negozio di calzature
shop *v* fare lo shopping
shopping lo shopping; ~ **area** la zona commerciale; ~ **centre [BE]** il centro commerciale; ~ **mall** il centro commerciale
short corto; ~ **sleeves** le maniche corte; **~s** i pantaloncini corti; **~-sighted [BE]** miope
shoulder la spalla
show *v* mostrare
shower la doccia
shrine il santuario
sick malato
side il lato; ~ **dish** il contorno; ~ **effect** l'effetto collaterale; ~ **order** il contorno
sightseeing la visita turistica; ~ **tour** la gita turistica
sign *v* firmare
silk la seta
silver l'argento
single (marriage) single; ~ **bed** il letto a una piazza; ~ **prints** le stampe singole; ~ **room** la stanza singola
sink il lavandino
sister la sorella
sit *v* sedersi
size la taglia
skin la pelle
skirt la gonna
ski *v* sciare; ~ *n* lo sci; ~ **lift** lo ski lift
sleep *v* dormire; **~er car** il vagone letto; **~ing bag** il sacco a pelo; **~ing car [BE]** il vagone letto
slice (of something) la fetta
slippers le ciabatte
slow lento; **~er** più lento; **~ly** lentamente
small piccolo; **~er** più piccolo
smoke *v* fumare
smoking (area) per fumatori
snack bar lo snack bar
sneakers le scarpe da ginnastica
snorkeling equipment l'attrezzatura da immersione
snow neve; **~board** lo snowboard; **~shoe** la scarpa da neve; **~y** nevoso
soap il sapone

soccer il calcio
sock il calzino
some qualche
soother [BE] il ciuccio
sore throat il mal di gola
sorry scusi
south sud
souvenir il souvenir; **~ store** il negozio di souvenir
spa la stazione termale
spatula la spatola
speak *v* parlare
special (food) la specialità; **~ist (doctor)** lo specialista
specimen il campione
speeding l'eccesso di velocità
spell *v* scrivere
spicy piccante
spine (body part) la spina dorsale
spoon il cucchiaio
sport lo sport; **~s massage** il massaggio sportivo
sporting goods store il negozio di articoli sportivi
sprain la storta
square quadrato; **~ kilometer** il chilometro quadrato; **~ meter** il metro quadrato
stadium lo stadio
stairs le scale
stamp *v* **(a ticket)** convalidare; **~** *n* **(postage)** il francobollo
start *v* iniziare
starter [BE] lo starter
station la stazione; **bus ~** la stazione dei bus; **gas ~** il benzinaio; **petrol ~ [BE]** il benzinaio; **railway ~ [BE]** la stazione ferroviaria; **subway ~** la stazione della metropolitana **train ~** la stazione ferroviaria; **underground ~ [BE]** la stazione della metropolitana; **~ wagon** la station wagon
statue la statua
stay *v* stare
steal *v* rubare
steep ripido
sterling silver l'argento massiccio
sting la puntura
stolen rubato
stomach lo stomaco; **~ache** il mal di stomaco
stop *v* fermarsi; **~** *n* la fermata
store directory la piantina del negozio
storey [BE] il piano
stove la cucina
straight dritto
strange strano
stream il ruscello
stroller il passeggino
student lo studente
study *v* studiare
stunning fenomenale
subtitle il sottotitolo
subway la metropolitana; **~ station** la stazione della metropolitana
suit l'abito; **~case** la valigia
sun il sole; **~block** il filtro solare; **~burn** la scottatura; **~glasses** gli occhiali da sole; **~ny** soleggiato; **~screen** il filtro solare; **~stroke** l'insolazione
super (fuel) la super; **~market** il supermercato; **~vision** la supervisione
surfboard la tavola da surf
swallow *v* ingoiare
sweater il maglione
sweatshirt la felpa
sweet (taste) dolce; **~s [BE]** le caramelle
swelling il gonfiore
swim *v* nuotare; **~suit** il costume da bagno
symbol (keyboard) il simbolo
synagogue la sinagoga

T

table il tavolo
tablet (medicine) la compressa
take *v* prendere; **~ away [BE]** portare via
tampon il tampone
taste *v* assaggiare
taxi il taxi
team la squadra
teaspoon il cucchiaino
telephone il telefono
temple (religious) il tempio
temporary provvisorio
tennis il tennis
tent la tenda; **~ peg** il picchetto da tenda; **~ pole** il paletto da tenda
terminal (airport) il terminal
terracotta la terracotta
terrible terribile
text *v* **(send a message)** inviare SMS; **~** *n* **(message)** il testo
thank *v* ringraziare; **~ you** grazie
that che
theater il teatro
theft il furto
there là
thief il ladro
thirsty assetato
this questo
throat la gola
ticket il biglietto; **~ office** la biglietteria; **~ed passenger** il passeggero con biglietto
tie (clothing) la cravatta
time il tempo; **~table [BE]** l'orario

tire lo pneumatico
tired stanco
tissue il fazzoletto di carta
tobacconist il tabaccaio
today oggi
toe il dito del piede; **~nail** l'unghia
toilet [BE] la toilette; **~ paper** la carta igienica
tomorrow domani
tongue la lingua
tonight stanotte
too troppo
tooth il dente; **~paste** il dentifricio
total (amount) il totale
tough (food) duro
tourist il turista; **~ information office** l'ufficio informazioni turistiche
tour la gita
tow truck il carro attrezzi
towel l'asciugamano
tower la torre
town la città; **~ hall** il municipio; **~ map** la cartina della città; **~ square** la piazza della città
toy il giocattolo; **~ store** il negozio di giocattoli
track (train) il binario
traditional tradizionale
traffic light il semaforo
trail il sentiero; **~ map** la mappa dei sentieri
trailer la roulotte
train il treno; **~ station** la stazione ferroviaria
transfer *v* **(change trains/flights)** cambiare; **~** *v* **(money)** trasferire
translate *v* tradurre
trash la spazzatura
travel viaggiare; **~ agency** l'agenzia viaggi; **~ sickness (air)** il mal d'aria; **~ sickness (car)** il mal d'auto; **~ sickness (sea)** il mal di mare; **~ers**
tree l'albero
trim (hair) una spuntatina
trip il viaggio
trolley [BE] il carrello
trousers i pantaloni
T-shirt la maglietta
turn off *v* spegnere
turn on *v* accendere
TV la TV
type *v* battere a macchina
tyre [BE] lo pneumatico

U

United Kingdom (U.K.) il Regno Unito
United States (U.S.) gli Stati Uniti
ugly brutto
umbrella l'ombrello
unattended incustodito
unconscious inconscio
underground [BE] la metropolitana; **~ station [BE]** la stazione della metropolitana
underpants le mutande
understand *v* capire
underwear la biancheria intima
university l'università
unleaded (gas) senza piombo
upper superiore
upset stomach lo stomaco in disordine
urgent urgente
use *v* usare
username il nome utente

V

vacancy la disponibilità
vacation la vacanza
vaccination la vaccinazione
vacuum cleaner l'aspirapolvere
vaginal infection l'infezione vaginale
valid valido
valley la valle
valuable di valore
value il valore
VAT [BE] l'IVA
vegetarian vegetariano
vehicle registration il numero di targa
viewpoint la prospettiva
village il villaggio
vineyard il vigneto
visa il visto
visit *v* visitare; **~ing hours** gli orari di visita
visually impaired ipovedente
volleyball game la partita di pallavolo
vomit *v* vomitare

W

wait *v* attendere; **~** *n* l'attesa; **~ing room** la sala d'attesa
waiter il cameriere
waitress la cameriera
wake *v* svegliare, svegliarsi; **~-up call** il servizio sveglia
walk *v* camminare; **~** *n* la passeggiata; **~ing route** il percorso pedonale
wallet il portafogli
warm *v* **(something)** riscaldare; **~** *adj* **(temperature)** caldo
washing machine la lavatrice
watch l'orologio
water skis lo sci d'acqua
waterfall la cascata
weather il tempo
week la settimana;

~end il fine settimana; **~ly** settimanalmente
welcome *v* accogliere
west ovest
what (question) cosa
wheelchair la sedia a rotelle; **~ ramp** la rampa per sedia a rotelle
when (question) quando
where (question) dove
white bianco; **~ gold** l'oro bianco
who (question) chi
widowed vedovo
wife la moglie
window la finestra; **~ case** la vetrina
windsurfer il windsurf
wine list la carta dei vini
wireless wireless; **~ internet** l'Internet wireless; **~ internet service** il servizio Internet wireless; **~ phone** il telefono cordless
with con
withdraw *v* ritirare; **~al (bank)** il prelievo
without senza
woman la donna
wool la lana
work *v* lavorare
wrap *v* incartare
wrist il polso
write *v* scrivere

Y

year l'anno
yellow giallo; **~ gold** l'oro giallo
yes sì
yesterday ieri
young giovane
youth hostel l'ostello della gioventù

Z

zoo lo zoo

ITALIAN-ENGLISH

A

a buon mercato inexpensive
a destra right (direction)
a girocollo crew neck
a notte per night
a settimana per week
a sinistra left (direction)
a tempo pieno full-time
l'abbazia abbey
l'abbigliamento clothing
abbracciare to hug
l'abito suit
accendere *v* light (cigarette); **~** *v* turn on (lights)
l'accendino lighter
accessibile ai disabili handicapped- [disabled BE] accessible
l'accesso access
accettare *v* accept
accogliere *v* welcome
l'acconciatura hairstyle
l'acconto cash advance
l'acqua water; **~ calda** hot water; **~ potabile** drinking water; **~scooter** jet ski
l'adattatore adapter
addebitare *v* charge (credit card)
l'aereo airplane
l'aeroporto airport
affamato hungry
affittare *v* rent [hire BE]
l'agenzia agency; **~ viaggi** travel agency
l'aggressione attack (on person)
l'agopuntura acupuncture
l'AIDS AIDS
aiutare to help
l'aiuto *n* help
al giorno per day
l'albero tree
all'angolo on the corner
allattare breastfeed
allergico allergic
l'alloggio accommodation
all'ora per hour
alto high
amare *v* love (someone)
l'ambulanza ambulance
americano American
l'amico friend
l'amore *n* love
analcolico non-alcoholic
andare *v* go (somewhere); **~ bene** fit (clothing)
l'andata e ritorno round-trip
l'anello ring
anemico anemic
l'anestesia anesthesia
l'animale animal
l'anno year
annullare *v* cancel
l'antibiotico antibiotic
l'antipasto appetizer [starter BE]
l'anziano senior citizen
aperto *adj* open
l'appartamento apartment

l'appendice appendix (body part)
l'appuntamento appointment
appuntito sharp
l'apribottiglie bottle opener
aprire *v* open
l'apriscatole can opener
arancione orange (color)
l'argento silver; ~ **massiccio** sterling silver
l'aria condizionata air conditioning
l'armadietto locker; ~ **dei bagagli** luggage locker
l'aromaterapia aromatherapy
arrivare *v* arrive
arrivederla goodbye
gli arrivi arrivals (airport)
l'arte art
l'arteria artery
gli articoli casalinghi household goods
l'artrite arthritis
l'ascensore elevator
l'asciugacapelli hair dryer
l'asciugamano towel
asmatico asthmatic
l'aspirapolvere vacuum cleaner
l'aspirina aspirin
assaggiare *v* taste
l'assegno *n* check (payment) [cheque BE]
assetato thirsty
l'assicurazione insurance
l'assorbente sanitary napkin [pad BE]
l'astuccio della macchina fotografica camera case
attendere *v* wait
l'attesa *n* wait
attraente attractive
l'attrattiva attraction (place); ~ **principale** main attraction
l'attrezzatura equipment; ~ **da immersione** snorkeling equipment; ~ **subacquea** diving equipment
gli auricolari headphones
Australia Australia
australiano Australian
l'auto car; ~**bus** bus; ~ **con il cambio automatico** automatic car; ~ **con il cambio manuale** manual car; ~ **a noleggio** rental [hire BE] car
automatico automatic
l'autonoleggio car rental [hire BE]
l'autostrada highway [motorway BE]
avere *v* have; ~ **la nausea** *v* be nauseous
avvertire *v* notify
l'avvocato lawyer

B

la babysitter babysitter
baciare *v* kiss
il bagaglio luggage [baggage BE]; ~ **a mano** carry-on [hand luggage BE]
il bagnino lifeguard
il bagno bathroom
ballare *v* dance
il ballo dancing
il balsamo conditioner
il bambino child
la bambola doll
la banca bank
il bancomat ATM, ATM card, debit card
la banconota *n* bill (money) [note BE]
il bar bar; ~ **per gay** gay bar
il barbecue barbecue
il barbiere barber
la barca boat; ~ **a remi** rowboat
il baseball baseball
il basketball basketball
basso low
i bastoncini cinesi chopsticks
battere a macchina *v* type
la batteria battery
il bebè baby
beige beige
bello beautiful
il belvedere overlook (scenic place)
ben riposato well-rested
la benda bandage
bene good
la benzina gas (vehicle) [petrol BE]
il benzinaio gas [petrol BE] station
bere *v* drink
la bevanda *n* drink
la biancheria intima underwear
bianco white
il biberon baby bottle
la biblioteca library
il bicchiere glass (drinking)
la bicicletta bicycle
la biglietteria ticket office
il biglietto ticket; ~ **del bus** bus ticket; ~ **elettronico** e-ticket; ~ **da visita** business card
il bikini bikini
il binario platform; track (train)
blu blue
la bocca mouth
la borsa bag
la borsetta purse [handbag BE]
il bosco forest
la bottiglia bottle
il box playpen
il braccialetto bracelet
il braccio arm
bruciare *v* burn
brutto ugly
la buca delle lettere postbox
buongiorno good

morning
buon pomeriggio good afternoon
buonasera good evening
buono *adj* good
il bus espresso express bus
la busta envelope

C

il cabaret cabaret
la cabina cabin
il caffè cafe, coffee
il calcio soccer
caldo hot (temperature)
il calore heat [heating BE]
le calorie calories
il calzino sock
cambiare *v* change; ~ *v* exchange; ~ *v* transfer
il cambio *n* change (money); ~ *n* exchange (place); ~ **valuta** currency exchange
la cameriera waitress
il cameriere waiter
la camicetta blouse
la camicia shirt
camminare *v* walk
campeggiare *v* camp
il campeggio campsite
il campione specimen
il campo field (sports); ~ **da golf** golf course; ~ **di battaglia** battleground
il Canada Canada
canadese Canadian
il canalone canyon
cancellare *v* clear (on an ATM)
il cane da guida guide dog
i capelli hair
capire *v* understand
il cappello hat
il cappotto coat
la caraffa carafe
le caramelle candy [sweet BE]
il carbone charcoal
carino cute
caro expensive
il carrello cart [trolley BE]; ~ **bagagli** luggage cart
il carro attrezzi tow truck
la carta card, paper; ~ **di credito** credit card; ~ **da cucina** paper towel; ~ **igienica** toilet paper; ~ **d'imbarco** boarding pass; ~ **stagnola** aluminum [kitchen BE] foil; ~ **dei vini** wine list
la cartina map; ~ **della città** town map; ~ **delle piste** trail [piste BE] map; ~ **stradale** road map
la cartolina postcard
il cartone carton
la casa house
la cascata waterfall
il casco helmet
il casinò casino
la cassa case (container); ~**forte** safe (for valuables)
la cassetta della posta mailbox
il cassiere cashier
il castello castle
la cattedrale cathedral
il cavatappi corkscrew
la caviglia ankle
il CD CD
Celsius Celsius
la cena dinner
il centimetro centimeter
il centro downtown area; ~ **business** business center; ~ **commerciale** shopping mall [centre BE]
la ceramica pottery
la ceretta wax; ~ **all'inguine** bikini wax; ~ **per sopracciglie** eyebrow wax
il certificato certificate
il cestino basket (grocery store)
che that
il check-in check-in (hotel/airport)
chi who
chiamare *v* call
la chiamata *n* call
la chiave key; ~ **elettronica** key card; ~ **della stanza** room key
la chiesa church
il chilo kilo; ~**grammo** kilogram; ~**metraggio** mileage; ~**metro** kilometer; ~**metro quadrato** square kilometer
chiudere *v* close (a shop); ~ *v* lock
chiuso closed
le ciabatte slippers
ciao hi, bye
il cibo food
il ciclismo cycling
il ciclo period (menstrual)
il cinema movie theater
cinese Chinese
la cintura belt
il circuito racetrack
la città town
il ciuccio pacifier [soother BE]
la classe class; ~ **business** business class; ~ **economica** economy class
il club club; ~ **di ballo** dance club; ~ **jazz** jazz club; ~ **per gay** gay club
il codice code; ~ **di abbigliamento** dress code; ~ **PIN** personal identification number (PIN)
la coincidenza connection (flight)
la colazione breakfast
la collana necklace
il collant pantyhose

il collega colleague
il collegamento connection (internet); ~ **wireless a Internet** wireless internet
collegarsi *v* connect (internet)
la collina hill
il collo neck
la colonia cologne
il colore color
il coltello knife
come how
il commissariato police station
la compagnia aerea airline
la compagnia di assicurazione insurance company
compilare *v* fill out (form)
il compleanno birthday
comporre il numero *v* dial
comprare *v* buy
la compressa tablet (medicine)
il computer computer
con with
il concerto concert
la condizione condition (medical)
la conferenza conference
confermare *v* confirm
la congestione congestion
il consolato consulate
il consulente consultant
contagioso contagious
i contanti *n* cash
contattare to contact
il conto *n* bill (of sale); ~ account; ~ **corrente** checking [current BE] account
il contorno side dish
controllare *v* check (luggage)
il controllo passaporti passport control
convalidare *v* stamp (a ticket)
la coperta blanket
il coperto cover charge
la coppa bowl
il corridoio aisle
corto short
cosa what (question)
la coscia thigh
costare *v* cost
costipato constipated
il costo charge (cost)
la costola rib (body part)
il costume da bagno swimsuit
il cotone cotton
il crampo mestruale menstrual cramp
la cravatta tie (clothing)
la crema cream (ointment); ~ **antisettica** antiseptic cream; ~ **da barba** shaving cream
il cristallo crystal
la cuccetta berth
il cucchiaino teaspoon
il cucchiaio spoon
la cucina kitchen, stove
cucinare *v* cook
la culla crib
il cuore heart
il cuscino pillow

D

da banco over the counter (medication)
danneggiare *v* damage
danneggiato damaged
dare *v* give; ~ **da mangiare** *v* feed
la data date (calendar)
del pomeriggio p.m.
il denaro money
il dente tooth
la dentiera denture
il dentifricio toothpaste
il dentista dentist
il deodorante deodorant
depositare *v* deposit
il deposito *n* deposit
derubato robbed
il deserto desert
il detersivo detergent; ~ **per i piatti** dishwashing liquid
di fronte a opposite
di valore valuable
diabetico diabetic
il diamante diamond
la diarrea diarrhea
dichiarare *v* declare
il diesel diesel
dietro around (the corner), behind (direction)
difficile difficult
digitale digital
la direzione direction
il disabile handicapped [disabled BE]
la disponibilità vacancy
il disturbo cardiaco heart condition
il dito finger; ~ **del piede** toe
divorziare *v* divorce
la doccia shower
la dogana customs
dolce sweet (taste)
il dollaro dollar (U.S.)
il dolore hurt (pain); ~ **al petto** chest pain
la domanda question
domani tomorrow
domestico domestic
la donna woman
dopo after; ~**barba** aftershave
doppiato dubbed
dormire *v* sleep
il dormitorio dormitory
dove where (question)
la dozzina dozen
dritto straight
durante during
duro tough (food)
duty-free duty-free
il DVD DVD

E

e and
l'eccesso excess; ~ **di velocità** speeding
economico cheap
l'edicola newsstand
l'edificio building;

~ **del parlamento** parliament building
l'effetto collaterale side effect
eliminare *v* delete (computer)
l'e-mail *n* e-mail
l'emergenza emergency
l'enoteca liquor store [off-licence BE]
entrare *v* enter
l'entrata entrance
l'erboristeria health food store
l'errore mistake
esausto exhausted
l'escursione excursion; ~ **in pullman** bus tour
esperto expert
espresso express
essere *v* be
est east
estrarre *v* extract (tooth)
l'età age
l'euro euro
extra extra; ~ **large** extra large

F

facile easy
la famiglia family
fare *v* do; ~ **l'autostop** *v* hitchhike; ~ **la ceretta** *v* wax; ~ **un incidente** *v* crash (car); ~ **il logoff** *v* log off (computer); ~ **il logon** *v* log on (computer); ~ **lo shopping** *v* shop; ~ **le valigie** *v* pack
la farmacia pharmacy [chemist BE]
il fast food fast food
la fattoria farm
la fattura bill [invoice BE]
fatturare *v* bill (charge)
il fax *n* fax
il fazzoletto di carta tissue
la febbre fever
il fegato liver (body part)
felice happy
la felpa sweatshirt
fenomenale stunning
fermarsi *v* stop
la fermata *n* stop; ~ **del bus** bus stop
il ferro da stiro *n* iron (clothes)
la fetta slice (of something)
il fiammifero *n* match (wooden stick)
il film movie
il filtro solare sunblock, sunscreen
il fine settimana weekend
la finestra window
finire *v* end
il fiore flower
firmare *v* sign
il fiume river
la fontana fountain
le forbici scissors
la forchetta fork
la foresta pluviale rainforest
il fornello da campeggio camping stove
la fortezza fort
la foto photo; ~ **digitale** digital photo; ~**copia** photocopy; ~**grafia** photography
il francobollo *n* stamp (postage)
il fratello brother
freddo cold (temperature)
il freezer freezer
i freni brakes (car)
frequentare to attend
fresco cool (temperature); ~ fresh
la fretta rush
il frigorifero refrigerator
la frutta e verdura produce
il fruttivendolo grocery store
fumare *v* smoke
la funivia cable car
il fuoco fire
fuori outside
il furto theft; ~ **con scasso** break-in (burglary)

G

la gamba leg
la gara di golf golf tournament
il garage garage
il gas gas (heating); ~ **per cucina** cooking gas
la gastronomia delicatessen
gay gay
il gel gel (hair)
gelato icy
il ghiaccio ice
la giacca jacket
giallo yellow
il giardino botanico botanical garden
il ginecologo gynecologist
il ginocchio knee
giocare *v* play
il giocattolo toy
la gioielleria jewelry
il gioielliere jeweler
il giornale newspaper
il giorno day
giovane young
la gita tour; ~ **turistica** sightseeing tour
il giubbotto di salvataggio life jacket
la giuntura joint (body part)
la goccia drop (medicine)
godersi *v* enjoy
la gola throat
il gomito elbow
la gomma rubber; ~ **a terra** flat tire; ~ **da masticare** chewing gum
il gonfiore swelling
la gonna skirt
i gradi degrees (temperature)
il grammo gram
grande big, large;

~ magazzino department store
grazie thank you
grigio gray
la grotta cave
il gruppo group
guardare *v* look
il guasto breakdown
la guida guide, guide book
guidare *v* drive

H

l'hockey hockey; **~ su ghiaccio** ice hockey
l'hotel hotel

I

l'ibuprofene ibuprofen
l'identificazione identification
ieri yesterday
imbarcarsi *v* board
l'impermeabile raincoat
in in; **~ pensione** retired
incartare *v* wrap
incassare *v* cash
l'incidente accident
incidere *v* engrave
incinta pregnant
includere *v* include
inconscio unconscious
incontrare *v* meet (someone)
l'incontro di boxe boxing match
l'incrocio intersection
incustodito unattended
l'indirizzo address; **~ e-mail** e-mail address
infastidire *v* bother
l'infermiere nurse
infetto infected
l'infezione vaginale vaginal infection
le informazioni information (phone)
inglese English
ingoiare *v* swallow
l'ingresso admission
iniziare *v* begin, start
inserire *v* insert
l'insetto bug
insipido bland
l'insolazione sunstroke
l'insonnia insomnia
l'insulina insulin
interessante interesting
intermedio intermediate
internazionale international (airport area)
l'Internet internet; **~ caffè** internet cafe; **~ wireless** wireless internet
l'interno extension (phone)
l'interprete interpreter
l'intestino intestine
intollerante al lattosio lactose intolerant
l'intrattenimento entertainment
inviare *v* send, ship (mail); **~ e-mail** *v* e-mail; **~ per fax** *v* fax; **~ SMS** *v* text (send a message)
ipermetrope far- [long- BE] sighted
ipovedente visually impaired
l'ippodromo horsetrack
l'Irlanda Ireland
irlandese Irish
l'irritazione rash
l'Italia Italy
italiano Italian
l'IVA sales tax [VAT BE]

J

il jazz jazz
i jeans jeans

L

là there
la casa prefabbricata mobile home
la stanza singola single room
il labbro lip
la lacca hairspray
il ladro thief
il lago lake
la lametta razor blade; **~ usa e getta** disposable razor
la lampadina lightbulb
la lana wool
il latte in polvere formula (baby)
il lato side
la lavanderia laundry; **~ a gettone** laundromat [launderette BE]
il lavandino sink
il lavasecco dry cleaner
la lavastoviglie dishwasher
la lavatrice washing machine
lavorare *v* work
il lavoro business
lentamente slowly
la lente lens; **~ a contatto** contact lens
il lenzuolo sheet
la lettera letter
il lettino cot
il letto bed; **~ matrimoniale** double bed; **~ a una piazza** single bed
la lezione lesson
libero available, free
la libreria bookstore
il libro book
il lift pass lift pass
la lima nail file
la linea line (train)
la lingua tongue
il lino linen
il litro liter
locale local
lontano far
la lozione lotion
la luce light (overhead)
il lunapark amusement park
lungo long

M

la macchina fotografica camera; **~ digitale** digital camera
il macellaio butcher
la madre mother
la maglietta T-shirt
il maglione sweater
magnifico magnificent
il mal sickness; **~ d'aria** motion sickness (air); **~ d'auto** motion sickness (car); **~ di gola** sore throat; **~ di mare** motion sickness (sea); **~ d'orecchio** earache; **~ di schiena** backache; **~ di stomaco** stomachache; **~ di testa** headache
malato sick [ill BE]
malattia sessualmente trasmissibile sexually transmitted disease (STD)
mancante missing
mangiare *v* eat
le maniche sleeves; **~ corte** short sleeves; **~ lunghe** long sleeves
il manicure manicure
la mano hand
il mare sea
il marito husband
marrone brown
il martello hammer
la mascella jaw
il massaggio massage; **~ sportivo** sports massage
il mattino morning
del mattino a.m.
il meccanico mechanic
la medicina medicine
il medico doctor
medio medium (size)
meno less
il menù menu; **~ delle bevande** drink menu; **~ per bambini** children's menu
il mercato market
le merci goods
il mese month
la messa mass (church service)
il messaggio message; **~ istantaneo** instant message
la metà half
il metro quadrato square meter
la metropolitana subway [underground BE]
la mezz'ora half hour
la mezzanotte midnight
il mezzo chilo half-kilo
mezzogiorno noon [midday BE]
il microonde microwave
migliore better
il migliore best
il minibar mini-bar
il minuto minute
miope near- [short- BE] sighted
misurare *v* measure (someone, something)
il misurino measuring spoon
mobile mobile
la mobilità mobility
i mocassini loafers
il mocio mop
modificare *v* alter (clothing)
il modulo form (fill-in)
la moglie wife
la moneta coin
la montagna mountain
il monumento memorial (place)
la moschea mosque
mostrare *v* show
la motocicletta motorcycle
il motore motor
il motoscafo motor boat
la mountain bike mountain bike
la mousse mousse (hair)
la multa fine (fee for breaking law)
il municipio town hall
il muscolo muscle
il museo museum
la musica music; **~ classica** classical music; **~ folk** folk music; **~ pop** pop music
le mutande underpants

N

il naso nose
il nastro trasportatore conveyor belt
le natiche buttocks
la nazionalità nationality
necessitare *v* need
il negozio store; **~ d'abbigliamento** clothing store; **~ d'antiquariato** antique store; **~ di articoli da regalo** gift shop; **~ di articoli sportivi** sporting goods store; **~ di calzature** shoe store; **~ di fotografia** camera store; **~ di giocattoli** toy store; **~ di musica** music store; **~ di souvenir** souvenir store
nero black
la neve snow
nevoso snowy
niente nothing
il nightclub nightclub
il nipote grandchild
no no
noioso boring
il nome name;

~ utente username
non fumatori non-smoking
il nonno grandparent
nord north
normale regular
la notte night
il numero number; **~ di fax** fax number; **~ di patente** driver's license number; **~ di targa** vehicle registration; **~ di telefono** phone number
nuotare *v* swim

O

gli occhiali glasses; **~ da sole** sunglasses
l'occhio eye
oggi today
OK OK
l'olio oil
l'ombrello umbrella
l'opera opera
ora now
l'ora hour
gli orari di visita visiting hours
l'orario schedule [timetable BE]; **~ d'apertura** business hours; **~ d'ufficio** office hours
l'orchestra orchestra
ordinare *v* order
gli orecchini earrings
l'orecchio ear
l'oro gold; **~bianco** white gold; **~ giallo** yellow gold
l'orologio watch; **~ da parete** wall clock
l'ospedale hospital
l'osso bone
l'ostello hostel; **~ della gioventù** youth hostel
l'ottico optician
l'otturazione filling (tooth)
ovest west

P

il pacchetto package
la padella frying pan
il padre father
il pagamento del conto check-out (hotel)
pagare *v* pay
il palazzo palace
la palestra gym
il paletto da tenda tent pole
la panetteria bakery
il pannolino diaper [nappy BE]
i pantaloncini corti shorts
i pantaloni pants [trousers BE]
il paracetamolo acetaminophen [paracetamol BE]
parcheggiare *v* park
il parcheggio parking garage; **~** parking lot [car park BE]
il parco *n* park; **~ giochi** playground
parlare *v* speak
il parrucchiere hair salon
le partenze departures (airport)
partire *v* leave
la partita game, match; **~ di football** soccer [football game BE]; **~ di pallavolo** volleyball game
part-time part-time
il passaggio lift
il passaporto passport
passare *v* pass through
il passeggero passenger; **~ con biglietto** ticketed passenger
la passeggiata *n* walk
il passeggino stroller [pushchair BE]
la password password
la pasticceria pastry shop
il pasto meal
il pediatra pediatrician
il pedicure pedicure
il pedone pedestrian
la pelle leather, skin
la pellicola per alimenti plastic wrap [cling film BE]
il peltro pewter
il pene penis
la penicillina penicillin
la penna pen
la pensione bed and breakfast
la pentola saucepan, pot
per for, per; **~ favore** please; **~ fumatori** smoking (area); **~ la notte** overnight
il percorso route; **~ alternativo** alternate route; **~ ciclabile** bike route; **~ pedonale** walking route
perdere *v* lose (something)
la perdita discharge (bodily fluid)
pericoloso dangerous
il periodo period (of time)
la perla pearl
permettere *v* allow, permit
perso lost
il pettine comb
il petto chest (body part)
il petto breast
il pezzo piece
piacere *v* like
il piacere pleasure
il piano floor [storey BE]
il pianterreno ground floor
la piantina del negozio store directory
il piatto plate; **~ principale** main course
la piazza della città town square
piccante hot (spicy)
il picchetto da tenda

tent peg
piccolo little, petite, small
il piede foot
il pigiama pajamas
la pillola Pill (birth control)
la pioggia rain
piovoso rainy
la piscina pool; **~ per bambini** kiddie [paddling BE] pool; **~ esterna** outdoor pool; **~ interna** indoor pool
pista piste [BE]
più more; **~ basso** lower; **~ economico** cheaper; **~ forte** louder; **~ grande** bigger; **~ lento** slower; **~ piccolo** smaller; **~ tardi** later; **~ veloce** faster
la pizzeria pizzeria
il pizzo lace
il platino platinum
lo pneumatico tire [tyre BE]
la polizia police
il polmone lung
il polso wrist
il pomeriggio afternoon
la pompa dell'aria air pump
il ponte bridge
la porta door; **~ antincendio** fire door
il portachiavi key ring
il portafogli wallet
portare *v* bring; **~ indietro** *v* return (something); **~ via** to go [take away BE]
la porzione portion; **~ per bambini** children's portion
la posa exposure (film)
la posta *n* mail [post BE]; **~ aerea** airmail
il posto seat; **~ sul corridoio** aisle seat
il pranzo lunch
la precedenza right of way
il prefisso area code; **~ del paese** country code
il prelievo withdrawal (bank)
prendere *v* take
prenotare *v* reserve
la prenotazione reservation
la presa elettrica electric outlet
prescrivere *v* prescribe
presentare *v* introduce
il preservativo condom
la pressione sanguigna blood pressure
presto early
la previsione forecast
il prezzo price
prima before, earlier; **~ classe** first class
primo first
il principiante beginner, novice
il problema problem
i prodotti per la pulizia cleaning supplies
profondamente deeply
il profumo perfume
il programma *n* schedule
programmare *v* schedule
proibire *v* prohibit
pronto ready
pronunciare *v* pronounce
la prospettiva viewpoint
prossimo next
provvisorio temporary
pubblico public
pulire *v* clean
pulito *adj* clean
la pulizia del viso facial
la puntura sting; **~ d'insetto** insect bite

Q

quadrato square
qualche some
la qualità quality
qualsiasi cosa anything
quando when (question)
quanto how much (question)
questo this
qui here

R

la racchetta racket (sports)
le racchette poles (skiing)
raccogliere *v* pick up (something)
raccomandare *v* recommend
la raccomandata registered mail
la raccomandazione recommendation
il radiatore heater
il raffreddore cold (sickness)
la ragazza girl, girlfriend
il ragazzo boy, boyfriend
raggiungere *v* reach (get hold of)
il rame copper
la rampa per sedia a rotelle wheelchair ramp
il rap rap (music)
la reazione allergica allergic reaction
la reception reception
il reclamo complaint
il regalo gift
il reggiseno bra
la regione region
il Regno Unito United Kingdom (U.K.)
la relazione relationship
il rene kidney (body part)
il repellente per gli insetti insect repellent
il residente UE EU resident

respirare *v* breathe
il ricambio part (for car)
il riciclaggio *n* recycling
la ricetta prescription
ricevere *v* receive
la ricevuta receipt
il riciclaggio *n* recycling
riempire *v* fill
rifiutare *v* decline (credit card)
ringraziare *v* thank
riparare *v* fix, mend, repair
ripetere *v* repeat
ripido steep
il responsabile manager
il riscaldamento heating
riscaldare *v* warm (something)
la riserva naturale nature preserve
i risparmi savings (account)
il ristorante restaurant
ritardare *v* delay
ritirare *v* withdraw
il ritiro bagagli baggage claim
la riunione meeting
la rivista magazine
romantico romantic
rompere *v* break
rosa pink
rosso red
rotto broken
la roulotte trailer
le rovine ruins
rubare *v* rob, steal
rubato stolen
il rugby rugby
il rullino film (camera)
il ruscello stream

S

il sacchetto per i rifiuti garbage [rubbish BE] bag
il sacco a pelo sleeping bag
la sala room; ~ **congressi** convention hall; ~ **d'attesa** waiting room; ~ **da concerti** concert hall; ~ **da pranzo** dining room; ~ **giochi** arcade; ~ **riunioni** meeting room
il salone di bellezza nail salon
la salute health
Salute! Cheers!
salvare *v* save (computer)
salve hello
la salvietta per neonati baby wipe
i sandali sandals
il sangue blood
sanguinare *v* bleed
il santuario shrine
il sapone soap
la sauna sauna
la sbornia hangover
le scale stairs; ~ **mobili** escalators
lo scanner scanner
le scarpe shoes; ~ **da neve** snowshoes; ~ **basse** flat shoes; ~ **col tacco alto** high-heeled shoes; ~ **da ginnastica** sneakers
gli scarponi da montagna hiking boots
la scatola box
lo scatolame canned good
scendere *v* get off (a train, bus, subway)
la scheda card; ~ **memoria** memory card; ~ **telefonica** phone card
lo schermo display
la schiena back (body part)
lo sci *n* ski; ~ **d'acqua** water skis
sciare *v* ski
la sciarpa scarf
la scienza science
scippare *v* mug
la scogliera cliff
la scolapasta colander
scollegare *v* disconnect (computer)
lo scollo a V V-neck
scommettere *v* place a bet
scomparso missing
lo sconto discount
lo scontrino bagagli luggage [baggage BE] ticket
lo scooter moped
la scopa broom
la scottatura sunburn
scrivere *v* spell, write
la scuola school
scuro dark
scusare *v* excuse
scusi sorry (apology)
sedersi *v* sit
la sedia chair; ~ **a rotelle** wheelchair; ~ **a sdraio** deck chair
il sedile per bambino child's seat
il seggiolino per auto car seat
il seggiolone highchair
la seggiovia chair lift
il self-service self-service
il semaforo traffic light
il seminario seminar
il senso unico one-way street
il sentiero path, trail
senza without; ~ **grassi** fat free; ~ **piombo** unleaded (gas)
separato separated (marriage)
la sera evening
serio serious
la serratura *n* lock
i servizi di pulizia domestica housekeeping services
il servizio service (in a restaurant); ~ **completo** full-service; ~ **di lavanderia**

laundry service; ~ **in camera** room service; ~ **Internet** internet service; ~ **Internet wireless** wireless internet service; ~ **sveglia** wake-up call
la seta silk
la settimana week
settimanalmente weekly
lo shampoo shampoo
lo shopping shopping
sì yes
la sicurezza security
sicuro safe [protected]
la sigaretta cigarette
il sigaro cigar
il simbolo symbol [keyboard]
la sinagoga synagogue
single single [marriage]
lo ski lift drag lift, ski lift
lo slip briefs [clothing]
lo smalto enamel [jewelry]
lo snack bar snack bar
lo snowboard snowboard
il sole sun
soleggiato sunny
solo alone, only; ~ **andata** one-way [ticket]
la soluzione per lenti a contatto contact lens solution
la sonnolenza drowsiness
sopra over
sordo deaf
la sorella sister
il sottotitolo subtitle
il souvenir souvenir
la spalla shoulder
la spatola spatula
la spazzatura trash [rubbish BE]
la spazzola hairbrush
lo specialista specialist [doctor]
la specialità special [food]
spedire *v* mail
spegnere *v* turn off [lights]
lo spettacolo *n* play [theater]; ~ **di danza** ballet
la spiaggia beach
la spilla brooch
la spina dorsale spine [body part]
spingere *v* push [door sign]
lo spogliatoio fitting room
sporco dirty
lo sport sport
sposare *v* marry
sposato married
la spuntatina trim [hair]
la squadra team
squisito delicious
lo stadio stadium
lo stagno pond
stampare *v* print
la stampa *n* print; ~ **digitale** digital print; ~ **singola** single print
stanco tired
stanotte tonight
la stanza room
stare *v* stay
gli Stati Uniti United States [U.S.]
la station wagon station wagon [estate car BE]
la statua statue
la stazione station; ~ **degli autobus** bus station; ~ **dei bus** bus station; ~ **ferroviaria** train station [railway station BE]; ~ **della metropolitana** subway station [underground station BE]; ~ **di servizio** gas station [petrol station BE]; ~ **termale** spa
la stecca di sigarette carton of cigarettes
le sterline pounds [British sterling]
stesso same
stirare *v* iron, press [clothing]
gli stivali boots
lo stomaco stomach; ~ **in disordine** upset stomach
stordito dizzy
la storta sprain
strano strange
straordinario amazing
lo studente student
studiare *v* study
stuprare *v* rape
lo stupro *n* rape
lo sturalavandini plunger
sud south
la super super [fuel]
superiore upper
il supermercato supermarket
la supervisione supervision
svegliare, svegliarsi *v* wake
sviluppare *v* develop [film]
svuotare *v* empty

T

il tabaccaio tobacconist
la taglia size; ~ **forte** plus size
tagliare *v* cut [hair]
il taglio *n* cut [injury], haircut
il tampone tampon
tardi late [time]
la tariffa fee
la tasca pocket
la tassa duty [tax]
il tasso di cambio exchange rate
la tavola da surf surfboard
il tavolo table
il taxi taxi
la tazza cup; ~ **di misurazione** measuring cup
il teatro theater; ~ **dell'opera** opera house

telefonare *v* phone
la telefonata phone call
il telefonino cell [mobile BE] phone
il telefono *n* phone; ~ telephone; ~ **cordless** wireless phone; ~ **pubblico** pay phone
il telone impermeabile groundcloth [groundsheet BE]
il tempio temple (religious)
il tempo time, weather
la tenda tent
il tennis tennis
la terapia ad ossigeno oxygen treatment
le terme hot spring
il terminal terminal (airport)
la terracotta terracotta
terribile terrible
la tessera card; ~ **associativa** membership card; ~ **dell'assicurazione** insurance card; ~ **internazionale dello studente** international student card
la testa head (body part)
il testo *n* text (message)
tirare *v* pull (door sign)
la toilette restroom [toilet BE]
la torcia elettrica flashlight
la torre tower
la tosse *n* cough
tossire *v* cough
il totale total (amount)
il tovagliolo napkin
tradizionale traditional
tradurre *v* translate
il traghetto ferry
tranquillo quiet
trasferire *v* transfer (money)
il travellers cheque travelers check [travelers cheque BE]
il treno train; ~ **espresso** express train
triste sad
troppo too
tuffarsi *v* dive
il turista tourist
la TV TV

U

l'uccello bird
l'ufficio office; ~ **di cambio** currency exchange office; ~ **informazioni** information desk; ~ **informazioni turistiche** tourist information office; ~ **oggetti smarriti** lost and found; ~ **postale** post office; ~ **prenotazioni** reservation desk
ultimo last
una volta once
l'unghia fingernail, toenail
unire *v* join
l'università university
uno one
l'uomo man
urgente urgent
usa e getta disposable
usare *v* use
uscire *v* exit
l'uscita gate (airport), exit; ~ **d'emergenza** emergency exit
l'utensile utensil

V

la vacanza vacation [holiday BE]
la vaccinazione vaccination
la vagina vagina
il vagone letto sleeper [sleeping BE] car
valido valid
la valigia suitcase
la valle valley
il valore value
la valuta currency
il vaso jar
vecchio old
vedere *v* see
vedovo widowed
vegetariano vegetarian
il veleno poison
veloce fast
vendere *v* sell
venire *v* come
il ventaglio fan (souvenir)
il ventilatore fan (appliance)
il verbale di polizia police report
verde green
vero real
la vescica bladder
il vestito dress (piece of clothing)
la vetrina window case
la vetrinetta display case
il vetro glass (material)
la vetta peak (of a mountain)
il viaggio trip
vicino close, near, nearby, next to
i vigili del fuoco fire department
il vigneto vineyard
il villaggio village
viola purple
la visita turistica sightseeing
visitare *v* visit
il viso face
il visto visa
la vita life
la vitamina vitamin
vivere *v* live
il volo flight; ~ **internazionale** international flight; ~ **nazionale** domestic flight
vomitare *v* vomit

W

il WC da campeggio chemical toilet
il windsurf windsurfer

Z

lo zaino backpack
la zona area; ~ **commerciale** shopping area; ~ **picnic** picnic area
lo zoo zoo

INDEX

Abbazia di Piona 48
Acquasplash Franciacorta 93
Alpyland Coaster 31, 92
Angera 35
Arona 35
Ascona 36
Bardolino 58
Baveno 30, 32
Bellagio 45
Bergamo 65, 91
Capella Colleoni 66
Duomo 66
Galleria Accademia Carrara 67
Borromeo Islands 28
Brescia 68, 86
Brunate funicular 41
Camonica Valley 63
Canevaworld 50, 93
Cannero Riviera 35
Cannobio 35
Castello di Vezio 47
Castiglione Olona 62
Cernobbio 41
Children 92
Como 37, 89
Basilica di San Fedele 39
Duomo 38
Museo Didattico della Seta 40
Cremona 71
Desenzano del Garda 49
Porto Vecchio 50
Villa Romana 49
Donizetti 68
Ferries 93
Franciacorta 64
Garda 48
Gardaland 50, 93
Gardesana Orientale 56
Gardone Riviera 51
Gargnano 53
Giardino Botanico Alpinia 31
Gignese 33
Goethe 57
Grotte de Catullo 49
Heller Garden 53
Il Vittoriale 52
Iseo 62
Isola Bella 28
Isola Comacina 43
Isola dei Pescatori 29
Isola di Garda 51
Isola Madre 30
Isola San Giulio 60
Isole di Brissago 37
Lake Como 37
Lake Garda 48
Lake Iseo 62
Lake Lugano 63
Lake Maggiore 27
Lake Orta 59
Lake Varese 62
Le Fontanelle 42
Limone sul Gard 53
Locarno 36
Lovere 63
Malcesine 56
Mantegna 74
Mantua 72
Menaggio 46
Milan 88
Monte Baldo 57
Monte Isola 62
Monte Mottarone 31
Monzino, Guido 43
Movieland Studios 50, 93
Museo della Bambola 35
Museo dell'Olio di Oliva 59
Museo dell'Ombrello e del Parasole 33
Museo del Vino 58
Museo di Comunale d'Arte Moderna 36
Orta San Giulio 59
Palazzo Tè 74
Pallanza 32
Parco Nazionale delle Incisioni Rupestri 64
Peschiera del Garda 50
Pisogne 63
Pliny 39
Punta San Vigilio 58
Ramo di Colico 48
Ramo di Como 41
Riva del Garda 54
Riviera degli Olivi 56
Rocca Borromeo 35
Rocca Scaligera 49
Sacro Monte (Orta San Giulio) 60
Sacro Monte (Varese) 61
Salò 50
San Carlone 35
Santa Caterina del Sasso 34
Santuario della Madonna del Sasso 36
Sarnico 63
Shakespeare Festival 87, 95
Sirmione 49
Strada del Vino Franciacorta 64
Stresa 27, 87
Torbole 56
Torri del Benaco 57
Varenna 47

Varese 61
Verbania 32
Verona 75
  Arche Scaligere 78
  Arena 76
  Casa di Giulietta 78
  Castelvecchio 81
  Loggia del Consiglio 77
  Palazzo della Ragione 77
  Piazza Brà 76
  Piazza dei Signori 77
  Piazza delle Erbe 77
  Roman Theatre 80
  San Fermo Maggiore 79
  Sant'Anastasia 80
  San Zeno Maggiore 81
Villa Carlotta 44
Villa Cipressi 47
Villa del Balbianello 42
Villa d'Este 41
Villa Le Fontanelle 42
Villa Melzi 46
Villa Monastero 47
Villa Pallavicino 32
Villa Panza 61
Villa Serbelloni 45
Villa Taranto 32
Virgil 74
Watersports 83

Berlitz pocket guide

ITALIAN LAKES

Fifth Edition 2019

Editor: Sian Marsh
Author: Susie Boulton
Head of DTP and Pre-Press: Rebeka Davies
Picture Editor: Tom Smyth
Cartography Update: Carte
Update by: Paul Stafford
Photography Credits: Alamy 88; Britta Jaschinski/Apa Publications 92; Fotolia 32, 34, 38, 76, 78; Getty Images 1, 4ML, 17; Greg Gladman/Apa Publications 6L; iStock 4TC, 4TL, 5T, 5M, 5MC, 13, 26, 46, 50, 52, 60, 62, 64, 75, 98, 102; Mary Evans Picture Library 15, 22; Neil Buchan-Grant/Apa Publications 7R, 11, 18, 42, 44, 48, 54, 56, 58, 66, 82, 85, 90, 101; Shutterstock 4MC, 5TC, 5MC, 5M, 6R, 7, 21, 29, 31, 37, 69, 70, 72, 81, 86, 94, 97; Switzerland Tourism 40
Cover Picture: AWL Images

Distribution
UK, Ireland and Europe: Apa Publications (UK) Ltd; sales@insightguides.com
United States and Canada: Ingram Publisher Services; ips@ingramcontent.com
Australia and New Zealand: Woodslane; info@woodslane.com.au
Southeast Asia: Apa Publications (SN) Pte; singaporeoffice@insightguides.com
Worldwide: Apa Publications (UK) Ltd; sales@insightguides.com

Special Sales, Content Licensing and CoPublishing
Insight Guides can be purchased in bulk quantities at discounted prices. We can create special editions, personalised jackets and corporate imprints tailored to your needs. sales@insightguides.com; www.insightguides.biz

Printed in China by CTPS

Contact us
Every effort has been made to provide accurate information in this publication, but changes are inevitable. The publisher cannot be responsible for any resulting loss, inconvenience or injury. We would appreciate it if readers would call our attention to any errors or outdated information. We also welcome your suggestions; please contact us at: berlitz@apaguide.co.uk
www.insightguides.com/berlitz